Has the Gay Movement
Failed?

ALSO BY MARTIN DUBERMAN

NONFICTION

The Rest of It: Cocaine, Hustlers, Depression, and Then Some (2018)

The Emperor Has No Clothes: Doug Ireland's Radical Voice, editor (2015)

Hold Tight Gently: Michael Callen, Essex Hemphill, and the Battlefield of AIDS (2014)

The Martin Duberman Reader (2013)

Howard Zinn: A Life on the Left (2012)

A Saving Remnant: The Radical Lives of Barbara Deming and David McReynolds (2011)

Waiting to Land: A (Mostly) Political Memoir, 1985–2008 (2009)

The Worlds of Lincoln Kirstein (2007)

Left Out: The Politics of Exclusion; Essays, 1964–2002 (2002)

Queer Representations: Reading Lives, Reading Cultures, editor (1997)

A Queer World: The Center for Lesbian and Gay Studies Reader, editor (1997)

Midlife Queer: Autobiography of a Decade, 1971–1981 (1996)

Stonewall (1994)

Cures: A Gay Man's Odyssey (1991; 2002)

Paul Robeson (1989)

Hidden from History: Reclaiming the Gay and Lesbian Past, coeditor (1989)

About Time: Exploring the Gay Past (1986; 1991)

Black Mountain: An Exploration in Community (1972; 1993; 2009)

The Uncompleted Past: Essays, 1962–1968 (1969)

James Russell Lowell (1966)

The Antislavery Vanguard: New Essays on the Abolitionists, editor (1965)

Charles Francis Adams, 1807–1886 (1961)

FICTION

Jews / Queers / Germans: A Novel/History (2017)
Haymarket (2003)

YOUNG ADULT

Lives of Notable Gay Men and Lesbians, editor (1994–1997), 10 vols.
Issues in Lesbian and Gay Life, editor (1994–1997), 4 vols.

DRAMA

Radical Acts: Collected Political Plays (2008)
Mother Earth (1991)
Visions of Kerouac (1977)
Male Armor: Selected Plays, 1968–1974 (1975)
The Memory Bank (1970)
In White America (1964)

Has the Gay Movement Failed?

MARTIN DUBERMAN

UNIVERSITY OF CALIFORNIA PRESS

University of California Press, one of the most distinguished university presses in the United States, enriches lives around the world by advancing scholarship in the humanities, social sciences, and natural sciences. Its activities are supported by the UC Press Foundation and by philanthropic contributions from individuals and institutions. For more information, visit www.ucpress.edu.

University of California Press
Oakland, California

Library of Congress Cataloging-in-Publication Data

Names: Duberman, Martin B., author.
Title: Has the gay movement failed? / Martin Duberman.
Description: Oakland, California : University of California Press, [2018] | Includes bibliographical references and index. |
Identifiers: LCCN 2017056078 (print) | LCCN 2017060440 (ebook) | ISBN 978-0-520-97084-7 (epub) | ISBN 978-0-520-29886-6 (cloth : alk. paper)
Subjects: LCSH: Gay liberation movement—United States—History. | Gay rights—United States—History. | Gay Liberation Front (New York, N.Y.)
Classification: LCC HQ76.8.U5 (ebook) | LCC HQ76.8.U5 D835 2018 (print) | DDC 306.76/60973—dc23
LC record available at https://lccn.loc.gov/2017056078

Manufactured in the United States of America

26 25 24 23 22 21 20 19 18
10 9 8 7 6 5 4 3 2 1

For Eli

O let none say I Love until aware
What huge resources it will take to nurse
   One ruining speck, one tiny hair
That casts a shadow through the universe.

W. H. Auden, "In Sickness and in Health"

True democracy begins
With free confession of our sins.
In this alone are all the same,
All are so weak that none dare claim
"I have the right to govern," or
"Behold in me the Moral Law,"
And all real unity commences
In consciousness of differences.

W. H. Auden, "New Year Letter"

Contents

Acknowledgments

My great thanks to Michael Bronski, Marcia Gallo, John Howard, and my partner, Eli Zal, all of whom have read the manuscript in its entirety; their wise suggestions were invaluable.

At the University of California Press I've been blessed with a dream team of talented specialists, and I very much appreciate their contributions: Kate Hoffman (project editor), Bradley Depew (editorial assistant), Peter Perez (public relations), Lia Tjandra (cover designer), and Jolene Torr (marketing manager). I'm profoundly indebted as well to Steven Baker for copyediting the manuscript with immense skill (including the upgrading of my primitive digital skills), and to Mark Mastromarino, who blessed me with a superb index. Above all I owe an enormous debt to my editor Niels Hooper for bringing me into the fold and for his sensitive, trenchant guidance throughout the entire process.

Prologue

.

VICTORY, the book cover shouts—and its tagline raises still higher the triumphalist beat: "How a Despised Minority Pushed Back, Beat Death, Found Love, and Changed America for Everyone."

Have we wandered into a revival meeting? No, *Victory* is one of several recent books, a whole new genre really, that portrays the improved public perception of LGBTQ people in hyperbolic terms skirting dangerously close to parody. Among other recent narrative histories that fall into the "triumphalist" camp—though less given than *Victory* to exaggerated tall tales— are Michael Klarman's *From the Closet to the Altar,* Jim Downs's *Stand By Me,* George Chauncey's *Why Marriage?,* Debbie Cenziper's *Love Wins,* and Nathaniel Frank's *Awakening.*

It is not wrong to claim that the past fifty years have marked a notable, even remarkable change in attitude toward sexual minorities in the United States. In the past half century we've gone from being all but uniformly pathologized and condemned—yes, even *hunted*—to being widely accepted as a legitimate minority (something like an ethnic one, though nobody seems sure). In 1950 fifteen states included us under their "sexual psychopath" laws, some of which defined "sodomy" as anal or oral sex with humans (with "beasts," too), and allowed indefinite confinement following arrest. Jumping forward fifty years, the U.S. Supreme Court has not only declared us "fit" for marriage but in 2003 decriminalized "sodomy" between consenting adults (more about that mixed blessing later), and in 2011 Congress repealed the military's grotesque "Don't ask, don't tell" policy. An improved status?—unquestionably yes. Yet the extent and content of our "progress" are badly in need of deconstruction.[1]

I'm not alone in feeling limited satisfaction with what most gay people are hailing as the speediest success story in all of our country's long history of social protest. The grumblers among us are a decided minority. We're overrepresented among gay academics and public intellectuals, but scarcely represented at all in the LBGTQ population at large. When complaining among ourselves, someone invariably cites the contrast between the movement's recent "assimilationist" agenda—marriage rights and "permission" to serve openly in the armed forces—with the far broader agenda that had characterized the Gay Liberation Front at its inception following the 1969 Stonewall riots. GLF had called for a fierce, full-scale assault on sexual and gender norms, on imperialistic wars and capitalistic greed, and on the shameful mistreatment of racial and ethnic minorities.

Or had it? Were we mythologizing the early years of the movement, exaggerating its scope in order to substantiate our discontent with what we viewed as the shriveled posture of the movement in its present guise?

In search of an answer, I took down a book from my shelves that I hadn't looked at in a very long time: *Out of the Closets: Voices of Gay Liberation,* the pioneering anthology that Karla Jay and

Allen Young, both of whom I knew, edited and published in 1972. Karla was at the time a graduate student at NYU and Allen had earlier been active in SDS (Students for a Democratic Society) and the Liberation News Service. Their anthology contained many of the crucial articles and manifestos that had emanated from the radical gay movement in its first three years of existence. I soon located a raft of other books from the period, including two additional anthologies Karla and Allen had edited (*After You're Out* and *Lavender Culture*).[2]

Many months of reading followed—along with a complex set of reactions, and somewhat more confusion than I'd anticipated. Yes, GLF had expressed empathy for nonconformists of varying stripes, had usually been clearheaded about our country's predations abroad and its indifference to misery at home (though GLF's rhetoric was sometimes more clamorous than its practice). And, yes, it had taken a generous swipe at traditional gender roles, the nuclear family structure, and lifetime, pair-bonded monogamy. Yet it had often done so at the top of its lungs, in utopian language of sometimes lofty (and stupefying) abstraction, and with more than a little self-righteousness. And like most left-wing movements for social change, GLF's internal debates had often been strident, with members frequently and passionately denouncing one another, often along gender lines.

Qualifiers aside, I came away from my self-imposed refresher course reaffirmed in my view that the modern gay movement in the period immediately following the 1969 Stonewall riots had indeed been broadly radical. It presented a substantive challenge to national values and institutions and was strenuously at odds with a merely "liberal" politics that simply called for integrating increasing numbers of people into what was purportedly a beneficent system. None of which came as much of a surprise, since I knew that many of those who joined GLF had earlier been energetically involved in the militant student, civil rights, feminist, and antiwar movements. A significant number of GLF recruits—people like Martha Shelley, Jim Fouratt, Ellen Shumsky (a.k.a. Ellen Bedoz), Michaela Griffo, Michael Brown, Karla and Allen—had previously marched on behalf of black rights, participated in early feminist protests, and joined actions against the war in Vietnam. The Stonewall riots had refocused their energies on gay liberation, yet in shifting priorities they'd maintained their prior concerns with racism, sexism, and imperialism.

The gay left—like every other kind of left in this country—has rarely represented more than a small minority. GLF and its less radical successor the Gay Activists Alliance (GAA) together probably numbered no more than a few hundred people—though more, doubtless, attended their dances. The straight left has periodically enlisted many more, with membership mushrooming during periods of uncommon economic hardship—like the Great Depression of the 1930s and the labor wars of the late nineteenth century—or in response to immoral foreign interventions (like the war in Vietnam). Yet once conditions improved, left-wing protest in this country has disintegrated with notable rapidity; it has historically failed to develop the sustaining power characteristic of the left in Europe.

If GLF's membership remained small, it spoke out against an impressive range of national shortcomings and hypocrisies. The group was quick to name the obstacles, such as racism and misogyny, that kept so many stalled on the first rung of the ladder, and it rejected the kind of patriotic sloganeering that served as cover for capital expansion overseas. As well, GLF deplored the embedded class structure that most Americans denied existed (even as it kept them locked in the cellar) and rejected, too, the claim that traditional notions of "maleness" and "female-ness" were biologically grounded—that our genes and hor-mones dictated and warranted the view that women were *intrin-sically* emotional and men *intrinsically* aggressive. Further, and centrally, the early gay movement affirmed sexual pleasure as a positive good, vigorously condemned the nuclear family as nothing more than a detention center for women and children, and viewed monogamy as unnatural.

Most of the radical young recruits to GLF had previously been in the closet in regard to their sexuality; they felt that now, in "speaking truth" about their own lives, they would forthwith be welcomed and would link arms with those telling the truth about racism, sexism, and unjust war—with the result of creat-ing a powerful political coalition that would refashion society as a whole. As the very first issue of the GLF paper *Come Out!* put it, "We are going to transform the society at large through the open realization of our own consciousness." To advance that goal, GLF stressed the importance of consciousness-raising groups.[3]

In giving voice to heretical views and denouncing what the vast majority of Americans (including most gay people) viewed as sacrosanct, GLF could sometimes be shrill, its analyses a jumble of simplistic, ill-digested notions, its views naively opti-mistic and at times downright Panglossian. Yet their dissent from established pieties, their passionate search for ways to alle-viate suffering, and not merely their own, still warrants our attention and regard. It's easy enough to mock their lapses into extravagant rhetoric, their wholesale indictments, their ingenu-ous sloganeering. It can be convenient too: by focusing on their sometimes chaotic antics, we're able to ignore as well the injus-tices they deplored.

The overwhelming majority of gay people, unlike those in GLF, remained closeted, their energy bent on avoiding detection. They sought to go unnoticed, to "get along," and they silently scoffed at those who blatantly paraded their dissent—or in the case of prominent earlier homophile activists like Frank Kameny or Barbara Gittings (genuine heroes in the context of what was possible in their own day)—openly deplored GLF's countercultural "nonsense." Yet in the face of widespread hostility, GLF persisted, somehow persuaded that a small group, if sufficiently dedicated and vocal, could set a generation's political agenda—or at the least plant the seeds for the later emergence of a larger progressive force. Vociferous and demanding, GLF announced the advent of a new kind of queer: boisterous, uncompromising, hell-raising.

Storming the Citadel

The Gay Liberation Front had originated in New York City following the 1969 Stonewall riots, but it spread quickly to a half-dozen other cities and college campuses in the United States—and had a particularly influential chapter in London. It was there that the Gay Revolution Party (GRP) issued a manifesto that envisioned a polyamorous sexuality freed from all association with procreation, and posited as well an ideal of androgyny—individuals combining in their persons the traits previously parceled out as intrinsic *either* to males *or* to females. A successful nonviolent gay revolution would be characterized, the GRP manifesto read, by the extent to which it did *not* "lead to straight-defined homosexuality with marriages and exclusive monogamy." Instead of fighting to gain entry to those antiquated institutions, the focus should be on expanding the scope of sexual expression for everyone. As Alan Sinfield would later put it, it wasn't the case of "an out-group need[ing] concessions, [but] rather the mainstream needing correction."[1]

One English publication in particular, a forty-two-page pamphlet entitled *With Downcast Gays: Aspects of Homosexual Self-Oppression,* still resonates above all others for its lucidity and perception.[2] It appeared in 1974, several years after GLF's heyday and perhaps profiting in clarity from the preliminary, more muddled discussions that had preceded. Its authors were the mathematician Andrew Hodges (later Alan Turing's biographer) and the artist David Hutter. The two announced at the top their primary purpose in writing the pamphlet with a quote from the London Gay Liberation Front Manifesto: "The ultimate success of all forms of oppression is our self-oppression. Self-oppression is achieved when the gay person has adopted and internalised straight people's definition of what is good and bad."

Unlike their GLF counterparts in the States, the authors of *With Downcast Gays* (*WDG*) focused less on social than on self-oppression, though the two inevitably comingle; as Hodges and Hutter succinctly put it, "We have been taught to hate ourselves." How so? Even as young children "we never hear anything good"—this was 1974—"said about gay life, and only see it referred to as a subject for mockery, disgust or pity." Reared "in alien, heterosexual nests," we grow up hearing the same message reiterated at home, and it's one that, inescapably, we come to internalize.

The vast majority of gay people manage to avoid or deny that fundamental fact, *WDG* goes on—which in turn explains why the ranks of gay liberation remain so thin; the vast majority of homosexuals remain "masochistically" detached from active protest. If cornered and challenged, if told that "it is society that must adapt to us, not us to society," they angrily deny their own oppression. "Like underpaid but genteel office-workers," Hodges and Hutter write, they "refuse to join the union. They prefer the imagined status that comes from identifying with the management"—an ahistorical yet telling retort to a gay movement that forty years later would put "marriage rights" at the top of its agenda.

WDC, in opposition, flatly rejected any and all efforts "to accept heterosexual conventions." The attack on gay male promiscuity as "sick" and "degenerate," the authors argued, should be met not with shamefaced apology, but with an expression of "pity for heterosexuals who find themselves trapped in an unhappy marriage." Gay men should "rejoice in the liberty their own homosexuality bestows," in the accessibility and ease with which they're able to make sexual contact and to avoid the "tedious process of persuasion—the ritualized escalation of intimacy to be carried out before sexual pleasure is reached." Nor was it true, Hodges and Hutter continued, that promiscuity was incompatible with forming lasting relationships.

But those relationships, they argued, were usually *not* carbon copies of durable heterosexual ones. Along with being more egalitarian and emotionally expressive, same-sex couples (so *WDC* asserted) "can identify with the sexual feelings of those they care for in a way logically impossible for non-gay people." In other words, a gay man can understand why his partner finds, say, that third man across the barroom attractive, and why he wants to bed him down. And why shouldn't he—or they—do so? To avoid jealousy? To avoid threatening the stability of the primary relationship? Both dangers can be negotiated—or long since have been (though the process can often be a good deal more fraught than Hodges and Hutter's somewhat airy confidence suggests).

Today a reader of *WDG* wonders, too, about the authors' blanket assertion that "it is easy for a gay partnership to develop into a non-sexual relationship in which the partners share loving companionship but find sexual pleasure outside the union—unlike many heterosexual marriages which turn into a boring embittered cohabitation in which sexual attraction has long vanished but fidelity is still rigidly enforced." Embedded in that sweeping contrast are a host of dubious or at least debatable claims—including the long-standing conundrum about how "natural" (or "unnatural") the relationship between love and sex is. Sidestepping that particular riddle for the moment, suffice it to say for now that some unknown but apparently significant number of *both* homosexual and heterosexual couples do seem to believe that sex is hottest with comparative strangers and love is the property of emotional trust and intimacy.

As for the "rigid" enforcement of heterosexual fidelity, males seem to ignore the directive often and with ease (even if recent research indicates that women are more lustful); for females, too, a woman's sense of sexual entitlement has grown exponentially since the 1950s. As for the current crop of Millennials (born between 1980 and 2000), the "hookup culture" has become something of a cliché—though the evidence that it brings satisfaction is to date mixed. One recent study concludes that 42 percent of never-married adolescents ages fifteen to nineteen say they have had sex at least once, and a 2013 Centers for Disease Control (CDC) report found that the number of high school students who reported having had sexual intercourse had actually decreased over the last decade from 47 percent to 41 percent. Yet a third survey suggests that twenty-somethings, too, are having *less* sex than their parents did, and with fewer sexual partners. In her 2016 book, *Girls and Sex,* Peggy Ornstein agrees that there's no evidence to suggest that the rate of young women engaging in sexual intercourse has risen in recent decades. What has changed, Ornstein argues, is that more young women are *performing* rather than *feeling* sensuality—and performing (faking orgasm) to please not themselves, but their male partners.[3]

The authors of *With Downcast Gays* would have been pleased to know that considerable evidence has accumulated to suggest the superior satisfactions associated with gay sex. Among queer women, according to one recent study, a growing number are indulging in polyamory (multiple, and simultaneous, relationships) *and* enjoying them a good deal more than their straight "hook-up" counterparts seem to be. What's more, the feeling of "compersion" (the opposite of jealousy)—that is, "shared delight in the compatibility of one's lover with someone else"—has become notable among white, middle-class, urban, and college-educated women.[4]

Such "sexual generosity" has long been known among gay men, though its frequency is much debated. Some forty years ago in *WDG,* Hodges and Hutter advocated "the eroticism of novelty in favour of the repressive dogma that sex is only satisfactory with one lifelong partner." "Puritanism," they claimed, "lies at the heart of the distrust of promiscuity.... Gay sex, unencumbered as it is with conception and contraception, could be [note: they don't say "is"] as free and available as sunshine and air"—obviously a statement that preceded the outbreak of AIDS—"and yet we are encouraged to disown these benefits in favour of the dubious respect gained by mimicking the outward forms of family life." *WDG* castigated those gay men—and there were many—who were urging gay people "to accept the claustrophobic restrictions of a life-long union. They are busily pushing us into the prison from which intelligent heterosexuals are trying to escape."

Hodges and Hutter were no less radical in their attack on traditional gender roles. Speaking for many male liberationists of the day—but most assuredly not all (or the lesbian contingent in GLF would not have felt increasingly alienated)—they rejected traditional concepts of masculinity and femininity, "with their respective associations of dominance and submission." Further, they advocated that gay men "should attack the idea that there is something wrong with effeminacy," while lesbians, comparably, should defend "butch" dress and mannerisms, pointing out that in the pre-Stonewall period it had been "camp queens and diesel dykes" who'd born "the brunt of heterosexual hatred." *With Downcast Gays* urged gay people to avoid trying to look like everyone else, trying to mimic "respectable" images—that is, "gratifyingly masculine or feminine" ones—and to adopt instead, even if the gesture initially felt awkward and artificial, "political drag."[5]

Though many gay men back then agreed with Hodges and Hutter that monogamy was unnatural and should be avoided, few volunteered to jump into frilly blouses and skirts (or whatever was regarded as currently appropriate female garb). My own lifestyle at the time is a case in point. Reading a newspaper interview I gave in 1977, I find that I echoed Hodges and Hutter's antipathy to "middle-class monogamy"; it's "not *my* preferred goal for the gay movement," I told the interviewer; "absolute monogamy," I went on, implicitly involves "the devaluation of sex" and considers "sex a destructive force unless it has the sanction of love." I further argued that gay men were "leading the way" in exploring a variety of sexual scenarios for themselves, in giving way "to a variety of impulses and moods."[6]

I gave my own sexual history as an example: "In my first relationship I felt I had to be the 'dominant' partner, to do all of the fucking because I had to imitate the straight male role. It took me years to overcome that, to overcome the feeling of compromising myself whenever I did play a 'submissive' role." In general I felt that "gay men know a lot more about sexual responsiveness, and the erotic potential of their bodies, particularly of their nipples and assholes, than straight men." I argued that "the discovery of submissive fantasies in males is one of the things gay people should stop apologizing for and begin to affirm." I believed that "we would automatically become a more potent force for changing society than we currently are, because we are presently often caught up in the process of denying the truth of our own experience, e.g.: claiming that we are just as macho-masculine as straight men, and no more promiscuous."

The extent of gay male promiscuity in the pre-AIDS seventies, even in New York City or San Francisco, can be exaggerated. A Kinsey Institute study published in 1978 estimated that roughly 20 percent of gay men (about the same percentage that chose celibacy) frequented the orgiastic frontiers—could in other words be accurately described as members in good standing of the sexual revolution. Yet at the same time—according to McWhirter and Mattison's *The Male Couple,* the standard work of the period—virtually all male couples had, after five years of being together, devised some formula that allowed for outside sexual activity. Hodges and Hutter would likely have hailed this as proof that when free to do so, couples discarded the artificial practice of monogamy. More recent studies, like *Sex at Dawn,* though attacked by some as "pseudo-science," have made the case for heterosexual couples adopting the same practice.[7]

AIDS, of course, changed the gay scenario. Yet some twenty years into the epidemic, and despite ample reason for fear, a number of studies from the early 2000s have reached a similar conclusion: though monogamy has gained more adherents than earlier, only between one-third and one-fourth of male couples together more than five years are sexually exclusive; the majority of subjects defined "fidelity" in terms of emotional commitment rather than sexual faithfulness—a much higher percentage than found among either lesbian or heterosexual couples.[8]

The Gay Liberation Front was organized around affinity cells, with people encouraged—in the anarchist tradition historically characteristic of this country's social protest movements—to congregate around their primary interests. Anyone could form a cell or join a new one. There was no application for membership, no paid staff, no dues—not even a constitution, bylaws, or mission statement. In New York the June 28th cell, for example, published *Come Out!* a community newspaper that had a substantial readership; the Aquarius cell planned the well-attended GLF dances; and the Red Butterfly cell described itself as "an association of revolutionary socialists" and concentrated its energy on "the class struggle" (John Lauritsen, along with John O'Brien, led the Red Butterfly cell and insisted, to deaf ears, that GLF should shed its anarchist tendencies and become a disciplined vanguard party). There was even a cell that—based on R. D. Laing's then widely fashionable *Politics of Experience*—announced that "paranoia is a state of heightened awareness."[9]

Every Sunday night the cells gathered for one large unstructured meeting in the basement of the Church of the Holy Apostles on Manhattan's West 28th Street. By lot, a new chairperson was chosen every month to run the meeting, with consensus (not majority vote) the guiding principle. Nothing remotely akin to parliamentary procedure or Robert's Rules of Order was followed, which made the achievement of "consensus" far from easy, and sometimes impossible, as defenders of the essential soundness of American institutions verbally battled self-styled revolutionaries calling for the destruction of the state.

A typical Sunday meeting at 28th Street would, at least intermittently, descend into chaos. When it did, it was often the men, exercising their sense of entitlement, who constantly interrupted and monopolized discussion. One central division among the male members was between those who emphasized the importance of consciousness-raising sessions to explore their own sexism and racism, and those who scoffed at such "bourgeois navel-gazing" and insisted on focusing instead on political activism. The two were not, of course, mutually exclusive; any number of GLFers went back and forth between self-examination and, say, "zapping" (successfully) the *Village Voice* for refusing to print the word *gay*.[10]

A number of GLF's public "actions" proved milestones. In the summer of 1970, a week after the murders at Kent State and the onset of bombing in Cambodia, a contingent of gay radicals invaded the national convention of the American Psychiatric Association (APA). They sat in on panels and presentations that ranged from the problem of Native American suicides (managing never to mention white genocide as a root causal factor), to the utility of aversion therapy in treating homosexuals (without considering the possibility that homosexuality wasn't in fact a "mental illness"), to the use of psychiatric "expertise" in assisting law enforcement (bypassing the issue of how society "uses police to oppress people and prevent change," as one of the protestors later put it).[11]

The radical contingent at the APA also heard Dr. Irving Bieber, professor of psychiatry at New York Medical College and a leading expert on homosexual "neurosis," once again recite his well-known theory of how a particular family culture produced male homosexuals: "Mothers of homosexuals are usually inadequate wives. They tend to dominate and minimize their husbands and frequently hold them more or less openly in contempt"—with the unhappy result that male offspring fail to identify with an appropriate male role model. Bieber's fellow expert, Dr. Charles Socarides, also gave a talk; he stressed that homosexuality was an emotional illness fraught with guilt and anxiety. That led Chicago's GLF to pass out a leaflet to the doctors in attendance asking if Socarides would "also consider Judaism an emotional illness because of the paranoia which Jews experienced in Nazi Germany?"[12]

When Dr. Nathaniel McConaghy of Australia began describing his success in giving homosexual male patients injections of apomorphine and then, while suffering from nausea, showing them slides of attractive males, the GLF attendees erupted. Joined by a group of some twenty feminists, GLF members jumped up from their seats in the auditorium with shouts of "Torture!" "Get Your Rocks Off That Way?!" and so forth. The disruption gave a number of psychiatrists pause, and it was only three years later that the APA voted, in a historic referendum, to drop homosexuality from the category of mental illness.

Not all gay activists liked being certified as "normal." Since the birth of the counterculture in the 1960s, a substantive challenge to the authority of the psychiatric profession had emerged and been gaining momentum. Among its gurus were R. D. Laing and Thomas Szasz, themselves psychiatrists, though highly critical of the profession's orthodoxy. Laing's best-known book was *The Divided Self* (1960), and the prolific Szasz turned out a number of influential works, including *The Myth of Mental Illness* (1961) and *The Manufacture of Madness* (1970).

Though the two men differed on much (for one thing, Szasz wasn't as inclusively anti-psychiatry as Laing), they agreed that what the profession called mental illness often wasn't an illness at all but rather a pattern of behavior that society found offensive and shocking. GLF couldn't have agreed more. It rejected the psychiatric emphasis on "adjustment," denouncing conformity in the name of liberation—liberation, for example, from antique notions of "normal" gender behavior. And GLF cited history to make the point: at least as far back as the mid-nineteenth century, women who rebelled against their subordinate status had been labeled "hysterics" and prescribed confinement to a rest home—a label, as the anti-psychiatry movement saw it, based not on any scientifically proven malfunctioning of the body but on unorthodox social behavior.

The gay radical press frequently cited Szasz and Laing when repudiating "normalcy" and asserting gay differentness—sometimes even *superiority*—to the mainstream. GLF occasionally carried the argument to a bizarre extreme—as in its claim, closely following Laing—that "schizophrenia is an experience saner than normality." New York's Red Butterfly collective provided a somewhat more sensible gloss: "Anyone growing up gay in America learns to develop a mildly schizophrenic personality style." Among the group of GLF men who called themselves Effeminists (the most prominent being Kenneth Pitchford and Steven Dansky) and who wholly supported a radical feminist agenda, Dansky spoke for them all in asserting that "the expression of political awareness is called madness by the patriarchy but ... can be recognized as revolutionary sanity by the oppressed."[13]

By the time the APA declassified homosexuality as an emotional illness in 1973, GLF as an organization had largely disintegrated, and most gay people greeted the news of declassification as a major breakthrough, the harbinger of still-greater approbation to come. It *was* a breakthrough—though only in the limited sense of marking a heightened tolerance for the notion that gay people *might* be viewed as eligible to join the ranks of mainstream respectability. That hadn't been GLF's goal: it saw its mission as challenging and changing mainstream norms, not complying with them.

Most of GLF's members in the early seventies were militantly anti-authority, whether that authority was embodied in the church, the state, or the medical profession. They denied the right of the courts, the clergy, or the psychiatric profession to pass judgment on their behavior or to "guide" it into the mainstream; they wanted their differentness acknowledged, not suppressed, wanted harassment and violence against them to cease. Not having sought approval from the APA mainstream, they gagged at its unexpected arrival. The news of having been declassified as "ill" was, as Abram J. Lewis has put it, "greeted on the gay left with an outpouring of sarcasm and indifference." Lewis quotes one gay student newspaper of the day as representative: the APA "has waived its magic wand and cleansed us, oh joy, of our dark and horrible sickness."[14]

The gay mainstream, however, *was* grateful, not angry. It regarded psychiatry's prior categorization of homosexuality as pathological as having been a scientific (not a moral) error—one that the APA had now corrected. In taking that position, the gay mainstream was in essence playing tit for tat: "You certify us as 'OK,' and we'll rehabilitate psychiatry as authoritative science." As Lewis has put it, "Declassification advocates leveraged their new publicity as an opportunity to speak with, rather than intervene against, psychiatric authorities."

Accordingly, during subsequent APA conventions, mainstream gays were *on* the panels rather than protesting them, as committed as the "experts" to believing the scientific method to be the true path to enlightenment. At the 1971 APA convention, pioneering activists Barbara Gittings and Frank Kameny not only served on a panel but distributed a leaflet attesting to the "proud and healthy constitutions" of gay people. As Lewis aptly comments, such a claim was tantamount to saying "that, as a group, homosexuals were uniquely impervious to their own oppression."[15]

GLF radicals, in contrast, insisted that gay people were *not* just like everybody else, and both Allen Young and Karla Jay were among those who resisted homogenization. Young wrote of his concern "about the resurgence of establishment values in the gay subculture," even within the gay liberation movement, and expressed skepticism about "self-acceptance achieved entirely on the terms of the dominant heterosexual order." Karla, for her part, hailed the developing lesbian separatist movement of the early seventies as voluntary disaffiliation not only from mainstream straight institutions and values but from "straight women and all men," and claimed it resulted in the flowering of a rich lesbian culture.

In general, lesbian feminists were far more vocal than gay men in arraigning the profession of psychiatry, along with most of the country's other male-dominated institutions. Within GLF, the large contingent of white men had from the beginning dominated the group's proceedings, despite the presence of some strong and contentiously radical women, including Martha Shelley, Lois Hart, and Karla Jay. A significant number of GLF's male members did respond to criticism, and in consciousness-raising groups sometimes took a searching inventory of their own sexism. But others among the men continued to patronize the GLF women—though few went as far as John Lauritsen later did when he made the claim that tension within GLF was due not to the sexism of the men but to the hostile attitude of the women, whom he accused of saying that the GLF men were "*more* sexist or *more* male chauvinist than straight men."[16]

In the face of persistent male chauvinism among some of the male members of GLF, the women members decided to form the Radicalesbians collective in the spring of 1970. Their founding document, "Woman-Identified Woman," famously declared that "a lesbian is the rage of all women condensed to the point of explosion," and described her as "in a state of continual war with everything around her, and usually with herself." Eschewing rationality and "balance" as the essence of "maturity," the Radicalesbians elevated outrage and fury as the appropriate emotions for combating the dehumanizing sexism long leveled against women. They regarded their perspective as superior to the heterosexual woman's demeaning compromises with male supremacy.[17]

GLF's Sunday night meetings were a raucous eye-opener for many who attended. Allen Young, for one, had been going to gay bars since the mid-sixties, but had "never been in a roomful of homosexuals where there was both laughter and serious conversation, and where the primary purpose was fighting for our rights." That meant, as Young put it, "identifying and rallying against those who oppressed us"—not merely established religion or the legal and medical professions but the media as well. They protested the way gay people were portrayed in the movies (as villains or clowns) as well as in print (mostly ignored or mentioned in association with criminal acts).[18]

GLF's concerns went considerably beyond gay issues themselves. The group was overtly anti-religious, anti–nuclear family, anticapitalist, and antiwar. As Young exuberantly put it: "The world feels new, as if it had just been created"—and was by implication open to a thorough inquisition and cleansing. He spoke for GLF as a whole when he characterized wars as "conceived and fought by men who are reared to play a 'macho' role." GLF wanted nothing to do with the armed forces and denounced the preceding homophile organizations for having included on their agendas the right of gay people to serve openly in the military (an issue that the movement would again feature after having turned assimilationist some two decades later).

Impressively—and again in contrast to the gay movement of recent decades—the young radicals in GLF were well aware of oppressions other than their own, and were especially vocal and demonstrative about racism. In her introduction to *Out of the*

Closets, Karla Jay, for one, wrote that "our struggle reflects the struggle of other revolutionary groups and of other oppressed people, such as the blacks, the chicanos, the American Indians, and women." She was sounding an "intersectional" note (to use the current phrase) that the Combahee River Collective, the black lesbian-feminist organization active in Boston from 1974 to 1980, would reiterate in even stronger terms in its now-famous "Collective Statement," a compelling insistence on the "simultaneity of oppressions" that refused to rank the relative impact of discriminations based on race, class, and gender. Some thirty years later, a number of mostly local groups—like Southerners On New Ground (SONG)—are again making the needed connections among the marginalized.[19]

Some GLFers, aware of the privileges that come with being white and middle-class, put their own oppression in perspective. As one of them, the film critic Stuart Byron, put it, "I consider the oppression experienced by a closeted gay white middle-class person … as a very privileged form of oppression compared to that experienced by a Latin American peasant or a black Mississippi sharecropper." In the years ahead, and until quite recently, the national gay movement would largely turn a blind eye to the plight of any marginalized group other than its own constituency.[20]

Some members of GLF even made a rather valiant attempt to apply GLF's radical views to reshaping their own lifestyles. In an effort to shed their middle-class backgrounds and habits, a number of GLF members joined collectives; Allen Young, for one, became part of the so-called 17th Street collective. Carl Miller, a recent graduate of the Rhode Island School of Design, was initially the moving force behind it; he had a spacious loft and decided to invite a small group of some half-dozen friends to share it with him. Along with Young, the group included Jim

Fouratt, who would become a force in the music industry; Giles Kotcher, later a pediatric nurse and the seller of modernist textiles; and Ron Auerbacher, who went on to become a holistic health practitioner. They slept on mattresses on the floor, did not have sex together, hosted gay visitors to New York, and wrote, published, and distributed a pamphlet series that they called "Gay Flames" (in honor of the odious term "flaming faggots").[21]

Not all was sweetness and light, however. Gay male sexism, an omnipresent issue from the earliest days of GLF, increasingly became the cause of bitter accusation and disgruntlement. The number of women in GLF was small in comparison to the male contingent (combined, only a few dozen people ever attended GLF meetings with any regularity), but they were a strong-minded bunch and never shy about accusing some of the men of being bad listeners, of repetitively, despite sharp correction, referring to women as "girls," and of interrupting at will when women were in the middle of a sentence.

Though many of the GLF men readily acknowledged their sexism and some worked hard at curbing it, others went right on interrupting and belittling, and a few "incorrigibles" insisted that the women were being oversensitive and that in fact *gay men* were *more* oppressed than the women because they were more susceptible to police arrest and mistreatment. While appreciative of the men who acknowledged and worked on their sexism, the women in GLF weren't about to accept or tolerate the recalcitrance of the others.

Some of the women felt caught between the devil (males in GLF) and the deep blue sea (the feminist movement). As Karla Jay put it, "Many lesbian/feminists were frustrated at feeling ignored by both the women's and gay movements." Even before Stonewall, a number of lesbians had enlisted in the feminist cause, though Karla, for one, had, after attending a few meetings, found NOW (the National Organization for Women), too tame, too focused on winning equal admission to an essentially unjust society. She decided to join the Redstockings instead, the cutting-edge radical feminist group that had started up in February 1969 and included such movement luminaries as Ellen Willis and Shulamith Firestone. Sympathetic to Marxist analysis, the Redstockings functioned as a group of semi-independent cells. A number of the women were heterosexual, and some of them brought along homophobic baggage from earlier affiliations with the Old Left—which was why Karla and other women decided to retain their affiliation with GLF instead.[22]

Many GLF men did think of themselves as feminists and strenuously supported the principle of gender parity. Yet their socialization as men meant that their actions sometimes belied their words—and even their intentions. They *wanted* to champion the feminist cause but—given the intractability of the adult psyche—couldn't always integrate their principles with their behavior. Yet they *did* sometimes succeed. The GLF group in Chicago, for example, issued a manifesto assailing "the whole package deal of inborn traits of women and of men" as "programmed role-playing" (what Judith Butler would later call "gender performance").

Sex roles, the Chicago manifesto insisted, had been so ingrained for so long "that 'normal' heterosexual relationships are so unequal, so exploitative, so possessive, so non-communicative ... that a ridiculously unloving standard of love is accepted." Women were treated, according to the manifesto, as an appendage—as ornament, toy, alter ego, parasite, burden, or slave." The Chicago group concluded that "gay liberation cannot be achieved internally while male supremacy and other sexist values remain within gay people, nor can it be achieved externally while sexist institutions remain intact." One male feminist in GLF–New York added that it was a myth "that heterosexuals have long and happy relationships which homosexuals can never achieve." Broadening the indictment still further, another GLF male added that "every man in Amerika is lonely, isolated, mistrustful and in desperate need of love. And everybody in Amerika is taught to hide his or her unhappiness at all costs."[23]

It's wonder enough that such radically egalitarian gender views were being sounded in GLF and that so many male members did strive to incorporate them in their daily lives. A worthy set of goals had at least been articulated; inevitably, the struggle to reach them would prove difficult and the results partial. Social transformation rarely follows a prescribed timetable—and never one that insists on rapid change. Inevitably, too, the gap between rhetoric and practice produces conflict and turmoil within the ranks of reformers, which then itself becomes a further obstacle to the kind of unified strength essential for embarking on a brave—or at least better—new world.

Like all of us, the GLFers of 1970 were products of their time and could never entirely free themselves of the wraparound tentacles of socialization. Yet they did something few of us ever attempt: they named what a better society might look like, thus establishing a standard by which to measure the alternating currents of progress and defeat. Refusing to excuse inertia by blaming immutable circumstance, they posited a commonality with other oppressed groups—and not just women—that sometimes patronizingly underplayed the gulf separating them, yet in the process managed to build some tentative foundations that, alas, have never yet been made solid.

Unlike the vast majority of people, this comparative handful of radical activists refused to soft-pedal their discontent or focus their energy on concealing their differentness. They countered the human wish to belong, to be seen as "just folks" and to be left alone to enjoy what limited comfort and safety was available in the face of daily discrimination and affliction, by actively engaging with the forces of oppression. Most gay people of their day dove for cover, scurried to conform, and desperately concealed every singular feature of their lives that might mark them as "other" and set them up as targets—a strategy easy enough to understand given the penalties and punishments awaiting those who spoke out. What makes a few defiant, and the rest submissive? We can't begin to know; *that* DNA will probably never be mapped.

Thanks to the scholarship of Christopher Phelps, we now know a good deal more than we once did about the attitude of Far Left organizations like the Socialist Workers Party, the Communist Party, and the YSA (Young Socialist Alliance) toward their gay members.[24] In the pre-Stonewall sixties they operated, as Phelps puts it in a nutshell, "as instruments of sexual repression." As early as 1951, Harry Hay, the pioneering gay organizer, had been dropped from Communist Party membership after revealing his homosexuality to the leadership, and other sexual "deviants" either retreated further into the closet or left politics altogether.

Though GLF's few Marxist-oriented members—most prominently John Lauritsen and John O'Brien—formed the group's Red Butterfly cell, they had few takers. Not only were the members of GLF, like most Americans, largely immune to Marxist class analysis, but many reacted badly to O'Brien and Lauritsen's tendency to treat their fellow gay activists as inferior in political acumen. Their claim that the Butterfly cell served as a kind of think tank for the movement had a certain merit: they did push for alliances with other groups working for social change, and they generated a number of useful pamphlets, including "Gay Liberation" and "Gay Oppression: A Radical Analysis."[25]

Moreover, the Red Butterfly collective agreed with most GLFers in their view of the traditional nuclear family. As one Butterfly pamphlet put it, "Women are possessed and oppressed by their husbands, and children by their parents"; it advised gay men and women to demand "freedom from being forced to mold their lives after a rigid, and strictly historical, family structure." As well, like everyone in GLF, the Red Butterfly cell defended homosexual acts as representing "natural, completely human forms of behavior," ones that occur "in a great variety of human societies." Unlike most members of GLF, however, O'Brien and Lauritsen claimed a "biological basis" for same-sex attraction. In this, the Red Butterfly represented what would become a common position: today, the biological explanation for homosexuality is (except for most gay intellectuals) very much the favored one.

When GLF adopted a series of motions declaring itself a "structureless structure" with decisions made not by voting but by consensus, the Red Butterfly cell defected, convinced that GLF had just committed suicide. Its departure wasn't widely regretted. Allen Young was among the many who were glad to see Red Butterfly depart; in his view, commonly shared, Lauritsen and O'Brien were bright and well informed but far too dogmatic for the free-wheeling give-and-take of GLF meetings.[26]

Carl Wittman's "Gay Manifesto," written a month before the Stonewall riots and in many ways prescient in its analysis, is probably the most notable of the pamphlets that Red Butterfly sponsored; still read and cited, it remains in both style and argument the most resonant piece of writing to have come down to us from the GLF period. The manifesto distills, sometimes eloquently, much of what can be counted as the gay male contingent's agenda for GLF—its arguments often more coherent than many members were themselves able or willing to articulate. As Simon Watney has pointed out, many members of GLF—in England as well as the United States—tended to see their ideological obligation discharged simply by denouncing anything that could conveniently be labeled "bourgeois" (though many were themselves products of the middle class). But being anti-bourgeois or anti-authoritarian, as Watney has justly said, can give way "all too soon [to] anti-rationalism and anti-intellectualism."[27]

One example is the view commonly (and glibly) held in GLF that being homosexual was *innately* subversive, automatically enrolling one as a *bona fide* "revolutionary"—as if the mere acknowledgement of same gender love and lust inescapably enrolled one in the radical ranks of those determined to overthrow the current "system" (itself cited far more often than analyzed). Comparably, the simple denunciation of a pernicious "gender system" isn't the equivalent of having carefully explored the content and process of being socialized into gender roles. Such systematic study or detailed discussion is notably absent from GLF writings, nor should that come as any surprise, since activism and scholarship rarely combine.

Carl Wittman's manifesto was more intellectually rigorous than most GLF publications, though a number of its assertions are employed as givens rather than as theories awaiting testing. Wittman starts off his declaration with a list of attributes *not* characteristic of male homosexuality: "It is not hatred or rejection of the opposite sex; it is not genetic; it is not the result of broken homes." Like all men, Wittman continues, gay men *are* chauvinistic—"we were brought up that way." The good news, as Wittman sees it, is that gay men could "junk it [male socialization] much more easily than straight men can. For we understand oppression ... our egos are not built on putting women down and having them build us up." Not so fast, many of the women in GLF might well have replied. That news is *too* good: in fact, understanding one's own oppression is no guarantee that you won't in turn oppress others. Besides, gay men, naturally enough, boost their egos wherever they can—and that includes ignoring or putting down their "sisters."

GLF women likely found Wittman's clear-cut take on traditional marriage more appealing: he straightforwardly denounces it as "a rotten, oppressive institution." Most straight couples, he argues, stay together for the presumed benefit to their children, to avoid their own parents' disapproval, and to maintain their reputation as upstanding citizens. Few gay people have any of that to lose. They, too, Wittman acknowledges, want "security, a flow of love, and a feeling of belonging and being needed," but they can get all that outside the bounds of marriage, "through a number of social relationships and living situations."

Those relationships, however, should, in Wittman's view, eschew "inflexible roles," "exclusiveness," "propertied attitudes toward each other [and] a mutual pact against the rest of the world." Specifically, gay people should enter relationships with no "promise about the future, which we have no right to make and which prevent[s] us from, or make[s] us feel guilty about" the kind of "growth" that multiple relationships, serially or concurrently, could offer. Wittman doesn't pause to explain his implicit preference for "multiple" relationships, nor how we might recognize when "growth" is or isn't taking place. Besides, aren't gay relationships, like any other kind, susceptible to exploitation, and, if so, what conditions and expectations should be encouraged or avoided to prevent that?

Along with renouncing marriage and monogamy, Wittman applauds adolescent sexuality. "Kids," he writes, "can take care of themselves, and are sexual beings way earlier than we'd like to admit ... those of us who began cruising in early adolescence know this, and we were doing the cruising, not being debauched by dirty old men." As for minority sexualities within the gay community, such as sadomasochists (or even those who cohabit with animals), Wittman urges us not to automatically denounce that which we neither share nor understand. He acknowledges that such sexualities "can be reflections of neurotic or self-hating patterns" but feels they might also be "enactments of spiritual or important phenomena"; for example, "sex with animals may be the beginning of interspecies communications." In any case, Wittman views "the harm done in these 'perversions' [as] undoubtedly less dangerous or unhealthy than is tobacco or alcohol" (though Wittman's dog may not have agreed).

As for politics, Wittman humanely cautions against the glib way current gay activists often denounce the preceding gay homophile movement as "reformist or pokey." He reminds his fellow radicals that those who'd participated in the earlier Mattachine Society and Daughters of Bilitis had taken grave personal risks in speaking out to any degree about the oppression that dogged their lives. Living in a different, deeply conservative time, they'd been the tiny minority with the courage to face down public ridicule—and punishment. Wittman—unlike many in GLF—also thought it essential for the gay community to focus its energy for the time being on the gay struggle itself. He urged support for the feminist and black struggles, "particularly when they are under attack from the establishment," yet believed that "right now the bulk of our work has to be among ourselves."[28]

Like many others in GLF, Wittman listed "capitalism" as among "our common enemies," but unlike most, he didn't pretend to know exactly what the term referred to or to have a clear perspective on what might replace it. He was clear that "as a group [we're not] Marxist or Communist," but he didn't feel that members had as yet "figured out what kind of political/economic system is good for us as gays. Neither capitalist [n]or socialist countries," he writes, "have treated us as anything other than *non grata* so far." For Wittman to admit uncertainty on some of the "big issues" was uncommon and even honorable, yet despite his own warning he sometimes alternates modesty with precisely the flat-out surety he otherwise deplores—as when he writes: "It's not a question of getting our share of the pie. The pie is rotten." Fifty years later, to be sure, radical gays—in tandem with lefties generally—still haven't filled in the blanks; self-labeling as "anti-capitalist" or "socialist" remains common, but concrete programmatic definitions, let alone strategies for implementing them, continue to prove elusive.

GLF as a whole did often sound a messianic note when discussing the need to wholly transform society rather than pleading for unconditional admittance to it (as had the preceding homophile movement). GLF saw itself as part of the broader movement for social change then convulsing the country and typified by the antiwar, black, feminist, indigenous, and New Left protests. Yet, when it came down to supporting particular struggles—in particular the Black Panthers and the Cuban revolution—GLF found itself internally riven by prolonged, heated debate. Carl Wittman, for one, had rejected the view strenuously held by some GLF members that the gay liberation movement ought to give high priority to the Panther struggle and to the Cuban defiance of American imperialism. The dis-

pute became somewhat more muted once it became clear that
neither the Panthers nor the Castro-ites sought support from
homosexuals—whom they in fact despised. Yet for a time the
pro-Panther contingent within GLF remained strong enough to
produce a considerable split in the movement.

A sizable number of the more moderate GLF men, and some
women (others shifted allegiance to the radical feminist movement), would eventually became frustrated enough with GLF's
chaotic climate of multiple causes and inconstant agendas to break
away in November 1970 and form GAA (the Gay Activists Alliance). The new group also comprised committed activists, and
included such prominent liberationists as Vito Russo, Morty Man-
ford, Arnie Kantrowitz, and Marty Robinson, but they insisted
that meetings adhere to Robert's Rules and set as their single goal
the achievement of civil liberties for gay people. GAA's formal
constitution stated in a bylaw that the group would not support
"any organization not directly related to the homosexual cause."

Preceding the GAA breakaway—and in part accounting for
it—the internal struggle within GLF over whether or not to
support the Panthers was for a time ardent and intense. In 1970 a
considerable contingent from GLF attended both a large antiwar conference held in Cleveland and the Black Panther Party's
"Revolutionary People's Constitutional Convention" in Philadelphia; the Panther convention drew some 15,000 people representing a host of left-wing groups that ranged from Women
Strike for Peace to the Weathermen. "There was a sense," as one
of the more radical members of GLF put it, "that the kind of
culture we wanted required so much change that it could only
be realized through revolution."[29]

In the weeks preceding the convention, Huey Newton
published in the Panthers' newspaper on August 21, 1970, his now-

famous letter "To the Revolutionary Brothers and Sisters," in which he referred to both homosexuals and women as "oppressed groups" and urged the Panthers to welcome them as such. "We must relate to the homosexual movement," Huey wrote, "because it's a real thing... homosexuals are not given freedom and liberty by anyone in society. Maybe they might be the most oppressed people in society." Most Panthers didn't see it that way. They freely referred to gay men as "faggots" and at least one GLF man, Jim Fouratt, tried for a time to justify the usage: eventually, he argued, the Panthers would have to be confronted on their homophobia and sexism, but for the moment they were, quite literally, under the gun, and he called for patience. (Soon after, Fouratt would himself openly criticize the Panthers for their homophobia at a rally in Hartford.)[30]

Nor did most Panthers appreciate the report that emanated from the convention's Male Homosexual Workshop, which declared "the revolution will not be complete until all men are free to express their love for one another sexually." As well, the report condemned the nuclear family as the fount of "the false categories of homosexuality and heterosexuality" and further insisted that "the social institution which prevents us all from expressing our total revolutionary love we define as sexism"— that is, the "belief or practice that the sex or sexual orientation of human beings gives to some the right to certain privileges, powers, or roles, while denying to others their full potential."

Though the Male Homosexual Workshop heralded the Panthers as "the vanguard of the people's revolution," the lesbian feminists at the convention begged to differ. They, too, called for "the abolishment of the nuclear family," but when they went on to decry "heterosexual role-programming and patriarchy," they were met with accusations at the convention of "racism and bourgeois indulgence." The Panthers in general viewed the traditional family as a bedrock of nurturance and support—and homosexuality as a symptom of Western decadence. During the convention Newton did not repeat his welcoming message to gay people, nor did any other Panther; they insisted instead that men, not women, were the movement's natural leaders. As if to prove the point, the convention voted to combine the lesbian workshop with the general "Women's Workshop" and denied it the right to issue an independent report.

A bitter Martha Shelley spoke for many lesbian feminists when she characterized the Panthers as believing women's function was to "bear revolutionary babies." The New York contingent of radical lesbians angrily left the conference before its close, and GLF's publication *Come Out!* subsequently denounced the Panthers as "sexist." Many retained sympathy with the Panthers' militancy, but at the same time felt that they were being "incredible pigs about women." Still, at the very next meeting of the People's Constitutional Convention in Washington, D.C., in late November 1970, some 150 gay men attended and some 700 women passed a resolution in support of the Panthers—signaling a willingness to set aside homophobia and sexism, for the time being, in order to foreground the black struggle.[31]

Allen Young was among the nonbelievers. His own history with the Cuban revolution had soured him on the possibility of straight left-wing radicals embracing the struggles of gay people and feminists. In the late sixties, when Young was still involved with the Liberation News Service and Students for a Democratic Society (SDS) and still closeted, he'd initially hailed Castro's successful overthrow of the Cuban dictator Batista—though acknowledging from the first that the new leadership was decidedly sexist. That, he felt, should come as no surprise, given Latin America's long-standing machismo culture; nor should it (as he wrote at the time) "prevent us from applauding the accomplishments of the revolution" in improving conditions of life for the average Cuban regarding health care, education, literacy, and diet.[32]

Young spoke Spanish and had earlier been a graduate student at Stanford's Institute of Hispanic American and Luso-Brazilian Studies. In 1969, before joining GLF and while still a member of SDS, he felt it was (as he put it) his "obligation to work to support Third World people who were opposing the military power and the racism of the U.S." Accordingly, he helped to organize a contingent of the Venceremos Brigades—a group of Americans who volunteered to cut sugar cane in solidarity with Cuban workers. Young went twice to Cuba—and the experience was a disillusioning eye-opener.

Along with experiencing venomous homophobia within the Brigades themselves, he found that homosexuals in Cuba had been denounced, expelled from schools, fired from jobs, denied admission to universities, and excluded from the political process. Young was told (as he later put it) "that homosexuality was an aberration produced under capitalism, that the future generations of Cuba would be free of homosexuals if only the youth of the country could be kept from having contact with acknowledged homosexuals." Thousands of gay people were forced into special agricultural work camps euphemistically known as Military Units to Increase Production (UMAP), and notorious for their bad conditions.

Despite some dissent, the New Left—dominated by macho-style young straight men—as a whole played down Cuba's homophobic policies, which led to considerable disillusion with the

Left among GLFers (as well as among straight women). The UMAP camps were dissolved in 1967, and since then life has slowly improved for gay people, but to this day machismo still reigns as the dominant ethos in Cuba. After 1970 the Venceremos Brigades themselves, dominated by members of SDS, denounced homosexuality as "a social pathology which reflects left-over bourgeois decadence" and banned gay men and lesbians from further participation.[33]

GLF's original Statement of Purpose, of July 31, 1969, had declared flat out that its members "reject society's attempt to impose sexual roles and definitions of our nature." But as always, rhetoric outran reality. The lesbian contingent expected macho hostility when working with the Panthers or the Cuban revolutionaries, but rightly refused to countenance it from straight women in NOW or from their gay male "brothers" in GLF. Lesbian activists came increasingly to feel that their best option might be to form their own separate organizations. In D.C. that conviction led to the famed Furies collective (which included Charlotte Bunch, subsequently a major theorist and organizer); in New York to the separatist group the Radicalesbians, whose influential founding statement, "The Woman-Identified Woman," noted that "as long as the label 'dyke' can be used to frighten women into a less militant stand, keep her separate from her sisters, keep her from giving primacy to anything other than men and family—then to that extent she is controlled by the male culture."[34]

As Charlotte Bunch emphasized, "Heterosexuality is a political institution." It embodies the heterosexist male assumption that women exist primarily to serve men—to carry their seed, bear and raise their children, run their households, meet their sexual and emotional needs. Women who stay in line do reap real, if delimiting, benefits of (as Charlotte put it) "legitimacy, economic security, social acceptance, legal and physical protection." Heterosexism regards as a "truism" that "heterosexuality is both the only natural and the superior form of human sexuality." Because gay men by their very existence—and sometimes by their renegade behavior—indirectly challenge straight male sovereignty, they've been historically derided and dismissed as pseudowomen.

Just as the primary aim of traditionalist women in the early seventies was to satisfy the needs and expectations of their male partners, so too, in GLF's view, did mainstream gay men pattern their behavior on that of straight men and bend their energies to winning their approval (and at least some access to their power). In doing so, they failed, GLF believed, to assert the validity, even necessity, of their own deviation from traditional norms—and in that failure fell by default into the enemy camp. To claim, as many mainstream gay men did, and still do, that nothing culturally distinctive follows from being sexually attracted to members of one's own gender, they were implicitly declaring the attraction an insignificant matter, like preferring a margarita to a martini; that was tantamount to "accepting things as they are," with the accompanying inequities and injustices either unrecognized or accepted as inevitabilities.

If these mainstream gay men became political at all, they mostly aimed, and mostly still do, at achieving all of the civil rights that adhere to first-class citizenship. Though GLF had no "reformist" wing, it did have some members who called themselves socialists and aligned their politics with the views of the straight left: capitalism was their prime target, not male chauvinism, and their allegiance to radical feminism was nonexistent or minimal. Further, they believed, if they acknowledged the issue at all, that homosexual oppression would inevitably collapse following the socialist revolution.[35]

The primary loyalty of some lesbian feminists was also to the Left; they ascribed their oppression not to male malignancy, whether deliberate or unconscious, but to a capitalist economy that oppressed women *and* men. Such women minimized the importance of "liberal" (NOW) issues like rape and abortion as of secondary importance to the traditional class struggle against capitalism and the moral struggle against racism. Alternatively, some lesbian feminists seemed to believe that the triumph of feminism would inescapably bring in its wake a victorious socialist revolution as well. Reformist feminists like Betty Friedan, in turn, warned that lesbian feminists in NOW would bring the entire movement into disrepute, and Roxanne Dunbar declared that "homosexuality is a chosen oppression whereas being a woman is the root oppression." The radical lesbian response was that their lack of dependence on men made them more likely to be woman-identified than were heterosexual women.[36]

The divisive lesbian-heterosexual split within feminism was paralleled by a comparable split between lesbians and gay men within GLF. In her introduction to the first edition of *Out of the Closets,* the 1972 anthology she coedited with Allen Young, Karla Jay acknowledged the internal struggles within GLF this way: "Gay men oppress gay women, white gays oppress black gays, and straight-looking gays oppress transvestites.... If we do share one idea, however, it is that gay is good." That one idea, it would turn out, wasn't enough to keep gay men and lesbians working together in the same organization.

It wasn't for lack of trying. And it wasn't for an entire lack of goodwill. Certainly there were gay men in GLF who felt, as one of them put it, that "the concept of gay liberation means nothing without an affirmation of the values of the feminist movement"— and that "gay liberation *with* feminism is the only logical solution to the problems we face as male homosexuals in this society." It followed that gay men and feminist women were natural allies against the culture's hegemonic insistence that there were only two genders, male and female, each sexually attracted to the other. One radical thread that ran through GLF was the call among some members to liberate same-gender desire in heterosexual men and women who insisted they were *solely* attracted to the opposite gender. (The trumpet was more muted regarding the obverse: that gay people, for their part, needed to liberate opposite-gender attraction within themselves.)[37]

Though many lesbians recognized the logic of an alliance with gay men, they nonetheless believed that women needed their own space—needed, in other words, to form their own organizations. Only an independent base, they argued, could neutralize their socialization as subordinates in a male supremacist world. The rejoinder of some GLF men was to claim that they were much more likely to support women's equality than was the male population at large. Which was true enough, though intentions, as a number of GLF women pointed out, too often outran practice—and a considerable number of gay men in GLF failed even to declare the intention.

Some GLF men did work hard in consciousness-raising groups on eradicating their privilege as men and on freeing themselves from conventional gender roles. The outer limit of GLF's willingness to commit to radical feminism was reached when three members—Steven Dansky, John Knoebel, and Kenneth Pitchford (the husband of radical feminist Robin Morgan)—formed the "Revolutionary Effeminists," began publishing the *Double-F* journal, and argued that gay men should virtually place themselves in the service of women, taking on their traditional household tasks, including the raising of children, in order to foster women's rise to power. Though the Effeminists' challenge to gender privilege was sometimes cogent—and other times opaque—their claim that sexism was at the root of *all* forms of oppression and the strenuousness of their assault on gay male culture went considerably beyond the tolerance level of most of the men in GLF, and the Effeminists succeeded in enlisting almost no one other than themselves.[38]

Besides, a number of "lifestyle" issues contributed to the growing alienation many GLF women felt from their male compatriots. Tension between the women and the men in GLF ran particularly high over the "correct" attitude to adopt toward sadomasochism. Though there were women who practiced it, the vast majority denounced it (at least verbally) as sanctifying and reinscribing the social roles of dominance and submission that continued to scar so many female lives. Few men in GLF openly laid claim to a predominantly S-M lifestyle, though now and then someone would rise to its defense, pointing out that oppressor-oppressed roles were endemic in the culture, straight and gay, and that acting them out in controlled, cathartic sexual rituals safely contained and minimized their presence in everyday life.

Besides, the proponents of S-M argued, the "dirtiest" secret about men, gay or straight, is that they *long* to be submissive. They're sick and tired of being in charge, of making the decisions, running the show (not a very persuasive description of most gay men's actual lot in life). They desperately, it was argued, want somebody else to take over, to give them permission to lapse into idle passivity. Everyone, the argument went, needs balance in their lives, and sex was one of the few available outlets for achieving it—a particularly complex, sophisticated outlet, one that primarily attracted creative, "highly imaginative" people desiring a constant heightening of sensation.[39]

"What crap!" was the prototypical feminist response (heard from almost all GLF women *and* most men). "Don't try to dress up sadomasochism as some sort of harmless pageantry or pretend that acting out dominant-submissive roles *de*creases the need to do so in real life." Sadism was quite simply, so the counterargument went, *cultivated* aggression. We shouldn't be a party to eroticizing violence as some sort of glamorous sidebar to so-called vanilla sex. If some people endow abuse with erotic power, they're to be pitied, not humored. Playing at humiliation underscores—it doesn't cure—low self-esteem; the repetition of a role doesn't diminish its hold, but entrenches it further. Besides, nobody "consents" to playing the masochist; the wounded ego, the disabled self, does the choosing.

Instead of eroticizing homosexual powerlessness, the counterview insisted, gay people needed to understand that contempt is not caring, bondage is not a prerequisite for freedom, nor brutality the messenger of love. S-M doesn't "liberate" anybody; humiliating someone doesn't—ten minutes later or ever—make them feel powerful, nor does it diminish the master's narcissism. What does get confirmed in an S-M ritual is the masculinist message that in a relationship one person *must* dominate. Besides, *no* rigid sexual role-playing can be called "liberated."

Yet another source of tension between the women and the men in GLF centered on transvestism (alternately called drag or cross-dressing). As one woman put it in the feminist publication *Sojourner,* "Drag is a blatant mockery of women, as genuine a manifestation of misogyny as the straight male practice of sexual harassment." An exception was made for "political" drag—for gay men who smeared on makeup, poured themselves into a trashy dress, and wobbled on high heels. That was considered a "gender-fuck" parody, a deliberately offensive challenge to traditional notions of femininity. What wasn't acceptable to many lesbians was the "genital" male genuinely trying to "pass," the male who felt most comfortable and "natural" when dressed in traditional female attire.

Part of the objection to transvestism was that, as one lesbian put it, "a man can take off his oppression as he pulls off his false eyelashes and his wig and his dress. But we wear it all our lives"—though in fact few lesbians at the time would have been caught dead in anything but jeans, a flannel shirt, and Birkenstocks. Nobody seems to have known back then that more married heterosexual men than gay men dressed at home in "women's" clothes—and brought along their wives to national cross-dressing conventions. Although Jan Morris (the well-known author of *Conundrum*) and a few others had already sought surgery to align (as they put it) their physiognomy with their psychology, the trans revolution was barely in swaddling clothes and only in recent years has the phenomenon shattered our binary notions of gender.

In my 1993 book *Stonewall,* one of the six people whose stories I tell is Sylvia Rivera, today widely hailed as a pioneering figure in the trans movement, along with her dear friend and fellow street hustler Marsha P. Johnson. I spent a good deal of time with Sylvia, recorded our conversations, and went on seeing her long after *Stonewall* had been published. Sylvia was active in GLF (though despised by some and feared by others), but she didn't fit neatly into the then-current definition of "drag queen"—or, for that matter, what we would today call a trans person.

For a short time Sylvia did take hormone shots (though she was never attracted to surgery) but then stopped. "I came to the conclusion," she told me, "that I didn't want to be a woman. I just want to be me. I want to be Sylvia Rivera. I like pretending. I like to have the role. I like to dress up and pretend, and let the world think about what I am. Is he, or isn't he? That's what I enjoy. I don't want to be a woman. Why? That means I can't fuck nobody up the ass. Two holes? No, no, no. That ain't goin' to get it. No, no, no."[40]

Sylvia did love drag, though usually confined it to face makeup and a loose blouse. She wasn't an entertainer, a female impersonator; she was, as she put it, "just a man who likes to dress up." Uniquely herself, Sylvia was a troubling figure to many in GLF, though more to the women than the men. Jim Fouratt and Karla Jay, unlike many others, liked Sylvia personally and admired her passionate insistence on speaking her mind and being herself. Jim thought she had a gut level understanding of oppression— more so than some of the theorizers in GLF. Karla, too, enjoyed her company, but felt the need to tell Sylvia that many of the women in GLF resented her wearing jewelry, makeup, and tight clothes—"exactly what women were trying to get rid of"; she was, in their view, copying and flaunting some of the worst aspects of female oppression. To which Sylvia would repeat, "I'm a man, not a woman. I'm just me, Sylvia."

Sylvia was ferociously loyal to GLF and, to a somewhat lesser extent, its more moderate successor, the Gay Activists Alliance (GAA). At one point she got the idea of creating some sort of refuge for the legion of homeless young street queens—at the time Rivera herself was all of nineteen—who often started hustling at age ten or eleven. She consulted with Marsha Johnson, and the two of them announced the formation of STAR—Street Transvestites Actual [soon changed to Action] Revolutionaries. Its first home was the back of an abandoned trailer truck, from which the group moved to an empty shell of a building on East 2nd Street. Sylvia organized a benefit dance for STAR, and GLF fronted her enough money to buy beer and setups. The dance was a success and Sylvia started to cook large dinners at night for "the children." But then one of the queens embezzled the rent money and STAR was evicted.

That didn't keep Sylvia—"completely stoned out"—from joining the GLF contingent that went to Philadelphia to attend the Panther's Revolutionary People's Constitutional Convention. There she ran into Huey Newton himself coming down a corridor, and he stopped to chat with her for a few minutes— which she regarded as one of the highlights of her life. Back in New York, she worked the night shift in a Jersey warehouse and took part thereafter in any number of GAA "zaps"—confrontations with homophobic public figures and organizations.

But by 1973, it all came crashing down. At that year's Gay Pride Rally, Sylvia, stoned on speed and booze, got up on the platform and grabbed the mike. Though one of the women from GAA wrestled it out of her hand, Sylvia managed a tearful shout-out about how the mostly white, predominantly male crowd wasn't doing a God-damn thing to help her sisters in jail, though it was the queens who'd been in the front ranks of the Stonewall riots. The crowd jeered and booed, eventually forcing Sylvia off the stage—and out of the movement. A true warrior for the rights of those who are "different," she never again found a place of comparable comfort.

Disagreement over gender issues was far more pronounced in GLF than those over race. On one level, race was a nonissue: no one mouthed the antiblack slurs all too common in general society and no one advocated banning blacks, Latinos, or Asians from membership. To the contrary, movement publications like *Come Out!* or *Fag Rag* fiercely indicted the country's entrenched racism and placed it on a par with imperialism as indelible stains on our democratic pretensions. In much of the white gay male world, on the other hand, racism was pronounced—even in regard to the bar scene: blacks, and to a somewhat lesser extent Latinos and Asians, were often "carded"—denied admission to clubs and, later, discos. This was *not* true, on a conscious level at least, of GLF, GAA, or the National Gay Task Force (which was founded in 1973 and which focused on civil rights issues). GLF, after all, did openly and strenuously support the Panthers and the Latino Young Lords—unlike many middle-class people of color. Yet Ron Ballard, an African American, was all but alone in consistently attending GLF meetings. If blacks were welcome in GLF, why did so few—indeed almost none—show up?

Part of the reason was undoubtedly an *un*conscious racism that most gay white people formally disclaimed but could nonetheless inadvertently exhibit; whites in GLF may have had trouble detecting their own prejudice, but blacks did not. Still, a full accounting for the absence of minorities in early gay organizations may be more intricate—may have to do with the very different attitudes radical gay whites and blacks had toward the nuclear family. Homosexuality seems to have been more acceptable to black families—"We don't throw our children away"—than to white, though with a qualifier: acceptable so long as the gay family member didn't constantly reference the fact or become "political" about it. Standing up for oneself about being black was one thing—about being gay quite another. As the gifted black gay writer Craig Harris put it, "Afro-American families relate well to homosexuality—as long as they can turn their backs on the issue.... [If] the homosexual family member decides to be political, or obvious in other ways, the family becomes confused, frightened, or disgusted by the display."[41]

And most gay black people weren't keen on alienating their families. "Home" was the one place where acceptance could be found, the only source of solace and comfort in a barren, hostile social landscape. When, somewhat later, more gay blacks became open about their sexuality, they tended—Black and White Men Together was a notable exception—to form their own organizations (for example, the Third World Gay Revolution, Salsa Soul Sisters, the National Coalition of Black Gays) and to publish their own magazines and journals (including *Blacklight* and the output of the Kitchen Table Women of Color Press). Tom Smith, who was African American, for a time served as the social and operations director of GAA—but was nearly the only black person in the organization; subsequently he became one of the founding members of the National Gay Task Force and for a time its director of finances.

Thomas Dotton was another African American who became active in the gay movement. As early as 1966, *before* Stonewall, Dotton allowed his name to be registered with the dean of Columbia College as one of the seven founders of the pioneering gay Student Homophile League. As he himself put it, "I gave myself unconditionally to the cause of gay liberation"—and in the process alienated himself "from the wider black community." "Only gay liberation," he would later write, "appeared to offer me freedom as both a black and a faggot."[42]

Appear is the critical word. Moving to the Boston area, Dotton soon came to feel that the gay world, too, "was unable to deal with Third World Faggots." Though the Boston-Cambridge axis contained what Dotton called "a large black and Latin gay community," it was "ignored by and of little interest to white faggots," and he came to advocate and participate in separate Third World conferences and organizations. "Whites will accuse us of 'separatism,'"

Dotton wrote, and will claim that "we blacks, Puerto Ricans, and others haven't the strength to stand alone." What they forget, Dotton bitterly added, is "just how alone we already stand within their movement."

From the start, GLF had strongly rejected traditional marriage bonds, denouncing the institution as singularly responsible for the "imprisonment" of women and children. In Karla Jay and Allen Young's *Out of the Closets: Voices of Gay Liberation* (1972), Young—anticipating by some forty years the view today common among gay radicals—warned against homosexuals ever opting for the "bad heterosexual institution" of monogamous marriage. Citing Herbert Marcuse's then-influential *Eros and Civilization,* which enunciated the concept of "repressive tolerance," Young warned against the tendency—today at flood tide—to co-opt homosexuals into "existing social norms, and hence reinforcing the latter." He acknowledged that "steady coupling" had its appeal as a stay against loneliness and a guarantee of companionship. He believed, too, that even in the early seventies, there were more long-lasting, "fairly monogamous" gay relationships among gay men and lesbians than usually acknowledged and thought they "resemble their heterosexual equivalents very closely"—just as he also believed that the extent of sexual promiscuity within the gay male world had been overestimated.[43]

All that said, Young continued to believe in the necessity of finding alternatives to the constraints of the nuclear family, and felt that the proliferation of both consciousness-raising groups and gay communes held out promise. In 1973 he would himself launch Butterworth Farm in rural Massachusetts, though the community soon broke apart. Still, he was pleased that in all the communes of which he had any knowledge, exclusive, possessive sexual relationships were considered undesirable; it suggested to Young that in a collective setting "there might emerge full and non-possessive sexual interaction—not necessarily genital—between all members." It was, to be sure, an idealized view of communal life that doesn't closely match up with the rather lugubrious history of such efforts, gay *and* straight, in this country. Yet in 2018 it's possible to see the recent appearance of nonpossessive polyamory among the young—along with a new insistence on gender fluidity—as just such attempts at creating inventive, more satisfying configurations of nonnuclear "families."⁴⁴

I know: what about kids—and who will take care of them? (leaving aside such standard communal issues as income—and jealousy). Not everyone thinks all children are adorable and loves being around them. I don't. In my darker moods I view them as demanding little bundles of narcissism. Even in my cheeriest ones I don't find—as so many adults seem to—their every squeal and gesture small miracles requiring repetitive oohs of admiration and transcending every need for adult communication. Yet even I believe that small children, in small doses, can be spellbinding. All right, then: why not the kibbutz solution? I'm aware of the disagreements over the outcome of that Israeli experiment and will cowardly plead the complexity of the argument, as well as its peripheral relationship to the marriage question I'm currently wrestling with, in order to back off from entering that debate.

However, I should at least add in my defense that around 1970 the gay baby boom was still a distant gleam and not even marginally discussed in connection with the marriage issue. A few gay men—and significantly more lesbians—did have custody of their children from prior heterosexual relationships, but I'm not aware of any statistics on the matter; in my limited reading in the

limited literature on gay communal life in the early seventies—
for example, Ray Mungo's mesmerizing *Famous Long Ago*—I don't
recall any mentions at all about who was minding the cribs (or
whether there were any).

As for the issue of same-sex parenting today, that once-con-
tentious debate seems concluded. Researchers at the University
of Melbourne found in a 2013 study that the children of same-
sex couples score 6 percent higher "than the general population
on measures of general health and family cohesion." The
stronger "family cohesion" apparently derives in large measure
from the fact that "work is more equitably distributed in same-
sex households ... [and] people take on roles that are suited to
their skill sets rather than falling into ... gender stereotypes,
which is mum staying home and looking after the kids and dad
going out to earn money."[45]

In 2016 the *Journal of Developmental and Behavioral Pediatrics*
reconfirmed the Melbourne study, finding that gay parents do
not disadvantage their children in any way: "The kids *are* all
right." Scientific consensus, of course, has never yet made a dent
in right-wing ideology, and the religious right continues to
regard same-sex parenting as destructive and immoral—just as
it continues to deny the scientific consensus on climate change.[46]

In 1970, issues relating to traditional child rearing and the
monogamous family unit were off GLF's radar—other than as
subjects of arraignment. There *was* some interest in countercultural experiments with communal living, and we hear echoes
of those debates today. Bella DePaulo's 2015 book, *How We Live
Now*, explores—and approves—a variety of nonnuclear family
configurations currently proliferating: collectives made up of
friends, not lovers; families that (by choice) contain several gen-

erations; polyamorous configurations that may or may not include shared housing.[47]

Reviewing DePaulo's book, the young journalist Hugh Ryan makes the central point: "Family isn't necessary—caring is." It reminds me of something I once read (though I can't recall its source) to the effect that a "successful" relationship is best defined not as one that sustains erotic intensity but rather one that helps to soften the brute fact that we're alone in this world—and will leave it. Ryan himself has lived polyamorously for five years with two male partners, and with six friends has recently bought a home together. He raises as well a central question: "If a family can have more than two adults, why can't a child have more than two parents?"[48]

Ryan shrewdly points out that "our community's ... mutable ways of loving one another are fast becoming something we need to defend all the more to the straight world—and, now, perhaps to our married gay peers as well." In citing his "community," he speaks of course of a comparatively small group of well-educated gay radicals whose constituency isn't much broader than one another. Which makes them more—rather than less—valuable. Ryan holds out the hope, which I share, that perhaps the radical left wing of the movement might yet persuade the larger gay community to reconsider "why our government is in the business of giving benefits to sexual relationships at all—gay or straight," and that someday these privileges will automatically adhere to individual citizenship.[49]

That's the echoey voice of GLF being sounded, reconfigured to suit the limitations—and options—of the present day. It's the same voice we heard from Lisa Kron, who wrote the book and lyrics for the Broadway musical *Fun House*, on hearing news of the Supreme Court's decision on same-sex marriage: "The thing I miss is the specialness of being gay. Because the traditional paths were closed, there was a consciousness to our lives, a necessary invention to the way we were going to celebrate and mark family and mark connection. That felt magical and beautiful."[50]

Pre-Stonewall activists who took part in the Mattachine Society and the Daughters of Bilitis—the so-called homophile movement that preceded GLF and GAA—never dreamt of demanding the legal right to marry; it would have been welcomed, but so would the Yellow Brick Road. Themselves creatures, like all of us, of the dominant social norms of the day, they in part shared them—more so than did the hippies or GLFers who came after—and in part grasped what was and wasn't possible and chose their battles accordingly. It *was* possible to inaugurate (not achieve) a campaign for equal citizenship; it was *not* feasible to challenge the contours or gain carbon-copy access to the ranks of "the American Family" and its tightly defined perimeters: male breadwinner, female hausfrau, two children. Homophile activists were (to use Gramscian terms) a "subaltern" pocket of resistance to *aspects* of the hegemonic culture in which they'd been raised and, in regard to some matters, they'd fully internalized its values and even seem to have felt guiltily inadequate at their inability neatly to fit the mold of "healthy" monogamous coupledom. A few somehow did manage it—more women than men.[51]

Unlike their homophile predecessors, many of the men in GLF refused to apologize for not conforming to mainstream patterns: they celebrated and indulged in the promiscuity available in bathhouses and elsewhere, and ascribed criticism of sexual variety to jealousy—especially from straight men locked into the "unnatural" prison of monogamy. Those who *did* acknowledge some degree of shame—including several men who were most vocal about the "wonders" of promiscuity—tended to link their multiplicity of sexual partners, quite irrationally, to an inability to form stable, intimate relationships (the shame itself the product of oppressive social conditions that had inculcated a sense of worthlessness). That was a minority view within GLF, though the question of whether "obsessive" promiscuity *was* the telltale sign of a personality disorder—and the guarantor of a discontented life—became the subject of some debate.

Though more of the women in GLF than the men came down on the side of limiting one's sexual partners, some of the women were among the most vocal defenders of "sexual variety." Rita Mae Brown, for one, expressed regret that sex for women—whether heterosexual or lesbian—was intrinsically bound up with "the old tyrannies of romance." She, too, wanted "the option of random sex with no emotional commitment" when in the mood for physical release, though she predicted that if women also had bathhouses, they would be "less competitive than the gay men's baths, more laughter would ring in the sauna, and you'd touch not only to fuck but just to touch." In any case, she wanted options, choices—"deep long-term relationships *and* short-term affairs"—and didn't regard the two as mutually exclusive (a view many radical LGBTQ people hold today).[52]

Another activist, Julie Lee, argued the issue from a different angle. Having lived in a monogamous relationship for more than twenty-two years, she'd come to feel that it was a practice designed to keep women enslaved. It bothered her that many of the women in GLF and even among the Radicalesbians denounced the practice of having more than one lover at a time as intrinsic to maleness, and she deplored their eagerness to support the "injured" partner and condemn the "guilty" one. As Lee saw it, "monogamy—as we understand it in our culture—

takes two individuals and molds them into one unit, then kills the individual, including that individual's needs, wants, desires, and independent action." She puzzled over why some lesbians, outlaws in many ways, were drawn to defending the hidebound institution of monogamy. She thought part of the answer was "security"; most people, Lee decided, "need someone to be with, to be close to, to live with, to love and to feel part of," but the need itself, she felt, was strictly the result of having been socialized as women. (Others would want to argue that the need is universal.) She felt, too, that some gay men and women who did form stable couples were driven by the need to gain at least a modicum of social approval.[53]

The lifestyle issues contested in GLF usually ran along gender lines. The men *tended*—the division was not absolute—to privilege the countercultural emphasis on "sexual liberation," while *somewhat* more women than men insisted on focusing on a political agenda that aimed at "militant equality"—the end of "second-class citizenship." Many of the men in GLF saw no reason for an either-or choice; they moved easily between the anonymous sex bazaar in the Central Park "rambles" to angry street demonstrations. Gender differences continued to shade the choice of lifestyle. No women visited the rambles (nor any feminist-sanctioned equivalent), and many more women than men picketed with political signs demanding "equal pay for equal work."

What the new breed of gay male liberationists and Radicalesbian feminists strongly shared was a rejection of the politics of button-downed respectability that they felt had characterized the pre-Stonewall homophile movement—though that "respectability" has been overdrawn. Homophile groups were downright radical in their willingness to risk physical assault by annually picketing (starting in 1965) in front of Philadelphia's Independence Hall. To call the small group of pre-Stonewall activists "timid," as many post-Stonewall radicals did (and some historians still do), is to mistakenly equate a middle-class dress code with a refusal to stand firmly up for a just cause—a refusal that accurately characterized not the activists but rather the vast majority of their frightened and closeted contemporaries.

II

Love, Work, Sex

In contrast to the many members in GLF who denounced traditional marriage and monogamy, the national gay agenda of the past two decades has reversed course and all but exclusively concentrated on winning marriage rights for gay people (and, secondarily, the right to serve openly in the armed forces). Here is how Jim Downs, in his 2016 book *Stand by Me,* proudly traces the shift in priorities that has taken place over the past forty years: "Although legally prohibited, gay marriage developed as a popular ritual and tradition in the 1970s and became, in churches and synagogues across the country, the symbol of their new culture for many gay Americans."

Downs begins his tale of triumph in 1971, when Father Clement married his partner, John Noble, at the gay Church of the Beloved Disciple. Next up on the honor roll of heroes is the evangelical Reverend Troy Perry, founder of the Metropolitan Community Church, with its multiple branches, who in the early 1970s often officiated at gay marriages—though insisting that a couple stay together for at least six months before considering the ceremony.[1]

In the view of Downs—and apparently Clement and Perry as well—marriage and monogamy go hand in hand. Downs quotes with approval a member of the gay Catholic group Dignity who blames gay male sexual promiscuity in the seventies on a society that "almost seems to force us to be preoccupied with sex by setting us in a separate category *because* of our sexual orientation."

Downs doesn't list physical pleasure as even a tertiary cause for the proliferation of recreational sex.

He goes still further, claiming—in apparent reference to the early Seventies—that "the gay religious movement asserted themselves as a crucial part of the liberation struggle ... [and] made many inroads with gay political organizations." Really? *Which* part? Though it stands to reason that *some* members of GLF may have been, in varying degrees, religious, I haven't run across any pietistic references in the movement's literature. And GLF and GAA (Gay Activists Alliance) *were* the "liberation struggle"—certainly *not* the Church of the Beloved Disciple. If GLF or GAA did harbor a few members attracted to a religious faith, they would probably have known better than to announce the fact, since those organizations were overwhelmingly atheist or agnostic. GLF was bitterly opposed to organized religion, and in particular to Roman Catholicism; as Charlie Shively, editor of the radical publication *Fag Rag* put it, "Christianity is the enemy." He made a point of burning a Bible at the 1977 gay pride march in Boston.

Downs believes that too many people have mistakenly reduced "the history of the gay community in the 1970s ... to a night at the baths." His express purpose in writing the book, he tells us, was to demonstrate "that sex did not define gay [male] life." To achieve that end, I'm afraid, he's written what can only be called a sanitized history of the 1970s. I don't see how else one can read it—unless one wants to concentrate on the way it egregiously omits any discussion of the extent to which blacks, Latinos, and Asians were notable by their absence in the movement during that decade.

In regard to the issue of marriage, George Chauncey's *Why Marriage?* is a well-crafted, generally reliable history of the debate. It's also dotted here and there with statements that, taken together, encourage the Downs-like belief that every day in every way we've been getting better and better. When Chauncey claims that "antigay animus is not an artifact of human nature but a product of human history," we need to enter a cautionary note about too easily concluding that all "products of human history" can, given sufficient concentration, be changed.

Chauncey's view might seem unassailable, especially given the decline in homophobia over recent decades, but what is missing from the analysis is any acknowledgement of the phenomenon known as imprinting—the decisive and sometimes indelible stamp that early experience places on our subsequent behavior. When the imprinting is prolonged and implacable, it may well be impermeable to later efforts at alteration. No amount of mandated change will take hold if die-hard bigotry has been deeply ingrained in childhood; it obliterates rational capacity and bludgeons the moral sense. The attitudinal changes we've seen in recent decades regarding racism, sexism, and homophobia are real, but can encourage simplistic optimism about additional progress. Those changes may well have taken place among that segment of the population—we hope the largest one—never deeply drilled in bigotry as children.[2]

The combination of imprinting with the seeming intractability of xenophobia (intense, irrational fear of what is deemed "other") does or should make us at least *somewhat* skeptical about the inevitability of progress. Perhaps, the optimist may reply, we simply have to try harder. Perhaps, the pessimist will counter, no amount of effort can ever significantly dent the indelible human fear of the unfamiliar. In this argument, I come down on the side of the pessimist, though that goes against my temperament. I doubt we will ever wholly root out homophobia and misogyny in the world at large, not to mention antisemitism and

racism. Whatever chance we have of making a larger dent in bigotry in the future hinges on our awareness—rather than our
denial—of the obstacles. It won't do to parrot Andrew Sullivan's
glib remark of some years back that "the struggle for gay rights
is essentially over" (or words to that effect). "Victory" in any
totalizing sense is a chimera, one that elicits the average American's peculiar susceptibility to adolescent optimism.

In *Why Marriage?* Chauncey further declares that most gay
people will find—once they've come out—that "the gay world ...
[is] larger and more welcoming than they ever could have imagined." Is he saying this has long been the case or that it's a recent
development? Either way, I suspect, nonwhites, trans people, gay
adolescents, and women will take exception to the claim. Historically, blacks and Latinos were routinely "carded"—denied
admission—to white gay clubs; today, segregated socializing is
less pronounced but an expansively "welcoming" atmosphere
remains uncommon, and for trans people all but nonexistent.
Lesbian activists, comparably, have been subject through time to
gay male chauvinism so pronounced that they've felt the need
periodically to form separate organizations.

Chauncey has the sly habit—it's endemic in the historical
profession—of quoting other people to make his arguments for
him, thus avoiding the responsibility to claim them in his own
voice. In *Why Marriage?* he's particularly fond of quoting Evan
Wolfson, the founder and president of Freedom to Marry, the
organization more than any other responsible for propelling the
issue of marriage to the top of the gay agenda. He quotes Wolfson's words and, less frequently, those of other prominent
defenders of marriage, but without overtly declaring that he
shares their views (and certainly without challenging them).
This approach creates the inescapable impression, whether

Chauncey means to or not, that these pro-marriage spokespeople do speak for *him.*

"I'm not in this," Chauncey quotes Wolfson as saying, "to change the law. It's about changing society." No, his critics—I among them—respond, it's not about changing society, it's about *joining* society's mainstream, and on *its* terms. Wolfson is also quoted as saying that his goal is for "gay kids to grow up believing that they ... can choose the life they want to live." Chauncey gives that sentiment a little added boost in the very last line of *Why Marriage?* "As always," he writes, "our future lies in our own hands." It does? Who is being included in "our"? The assertion that we control our own destinies will come as a considerable surprise to the multitudes who have all their lives been dutiful citizens playing by the rules and toiling away at low-level jobs— and getting precisely nowhere. Most mainstream Americans will, thanks to their socialization, agree with Chauncey's bromide about how our fates are in our own hands. What inescapably follows is that they will blame themselves—not closed doors or glass ceilings—for failing to reach their goals, adding self-doubt and guilt to their already-heavy burden of social scorn.

In regard to the marriage issue itself, Chauncey announces in a throwaway line that "a full accounting of the gay debate over the desirability of marriage is beyond the scope of this book." He does acknowledge that the argument has been "fierce and wide-ranging" yet demurs from evaluating it beyond adding the spare, mysterious declaration that the debate "became captive" to divisions within the gay world. Which divisions? Why do we hear so little about the *anti*-Wolfson side of the debate? Instead of providing "equal time," Chauncey settles instead for reiterating Wolfson's pro-marriage arguments and denying any solid platform to his adversaries; Michael Warner's *The Trouble with Normal,* for example, a pathbreaking, incisive critique of the campaign to make same-sex marriage the central goal of the gay movement, is reduced to two sentences.

Wolfson obviously speaks for Chauncey, who not only cites him at length but never criticizes the content of his advocacy—even when a rejoinder seems obvious and necessary. Thus Chauncey quotes at length Wolfson's defense of traditional marriage as providing "a vocabulary in which non-gay people talk about larger important questions—questions of love and commitment and dedication and self-sacrifice and family, but also equality and participation and connectedness"—making it clear that he and Wolfson want to claim that vocabulary for themselves, and think all gay people should. Why? Because it would "make it easier for non-gay people to understand who we are."

Sorry, but that strikes me as an intellectual version of three-card monte. What Wolfson and Chauncey are irreducibly advocating, consciously or not, is that we become *like* straight people—that we adopt their vocabulary (a code word for their way of life). What's more, it's *our* responsibility to make ourselves more intelligible, not *theirs* to understand our differentness (which in any case Chauncey apparently considers minimal). The main goal here is to make ourselves "familiar enough" to straight people to win their acceptance. But why should *that* be of paramount importance? Precisely why would we want to do ourselves over in their image? To become more like them would be to forget our own singular history and the special insights and perspectives that derive from it, giving us, as spies in the culture, a unique perspective for evaluating and critiquing aspects of mainstream culture.

Chauncey and Wolfson are in essence telling us—though never directly—to suppress whatever makes us special, to deny that we have a unique contribution to make to the mainstream's understanding of itself, and to spend our energies instead on pretending—sometimes to ourselves—that we're "just folks," with the same desires and values all the good people who inhabit coupled middle-class America share. If we would only agree with Wolfson and Chauncey that marriage, as they put it, "brings clarity and security" and stop harping on our differentness, we could throw off the bonds of second-class citizenship.

When they declare that gay marriage will bring us "clarity and security," what sort of clarity do they have in mind? Not the sort, apparently, that makes our differentness from mainstream culture transparently obvious—like the *fact* that historically we've been more open to sexual innovation and pleasure, to mutuality in our partnerships, and to nontraditional forms of gender identity, than have our straight counterparts. No, the essential Wolfson-Chauncey position is, in sum: assimilate—follow the example many Jews set in Weimar Germany: adapt to mainstream norms. To his credit, Chauncey does cite theorists of ethnicity who leave open the possibility that even as immigrants and outsiders have been "reshaped by their incorporation into American culture," so too has the culture itself been changed by the process. That possibility is a real one, and can be certified historically. Yet a possibility is not a guarantee; much depends on the amount of pressure outsiders are capable—and desirous—of bringing to bear. Many Jews did blend in, or thought they had. Yet German antisemitism was to no extent changed or diminished—and neither clarity nor security followed.

Something more needs to be said about the closing line in Chauncey's book: "Our future lies in our own hands." At the heart of that assertion lies the most deceptive and corrosive doctrine in our country's ideological arsenal: that our own history or the country's current norms haven't to any degree preformed (and deformed) our available options, that we are entirely free to proceed in life as we choose. Try telling that to blacks, poor people, and women. Or try insisting that anyone who applies themselves with sufficient determination can achieve whatever it is they desire. Work hard, clarify your goals, pursue them tenaciously, and it will follow as the night the day—or so the Chauncey-ites imply—that you will reach your goal. Put another way, if we *don't* fulfill our dreams, we have only ourselves to blame, since no pre-existing obstacles have blocked our path or limited our options. It's an analysis that *perhaps* describes those few who are born into privilege or have extraordinary gifts—but that automatically leaves out the vast majority.

Yet there it is—the absolute essence of what we call "the American Dream": the hoary adage that you can pull yourself up by your own bootstraps. Yet as James Surowiecki pointed out a few years back, recent studies show that although social mobility "remained relatively stable over the entire second half of the twentieth century ... there wasn't that much mobility to begin with"—and there's less of it than in most European countries. There *was* considerable mobility in the late nineteenth century—and *more* than in Europe. The average American worker's assumption back then that he had a reasonably good chance of rising out of his class was accurate. Unfortunately, that assumption has continued to hold sway while the reality has shifted. Today, according to Surowiecki, "seventy percent of people born into the bottom quintile never make it into the middle class."[3]

Yet the sloganeering about upward mobility continues, made more offensive still by the wage stagnation of recent decades and the resulting decline in the average American's standard of living. As Michael Harrington wrote way back in 1962 in *The Other America*, the primary reason most people remain poor is that "they made the mistake of being born to the wrong parents"—into families that faced built-in obstacles to advancement based on race, class, and gender. Those are the real forces that determine the nature of your journey through life, though that's not how our official ideology tells the story, a story most Americans internalize at an early age: only *you* stand in the way of your own success.

Which is also the false doctrine at the heart of American "liberalism," the notion more responsible than any other aspect of our official ideology for having sapped the strength of every movement for social reform in our history: if individuals are alone responsible for their own fate, there's no warrant for troubling deaf heaven with claims about the "unfairness" of the system. Our institutional structure, so goes the argument, is essentially benign—and our society welcoming to all those who believe in its values and work hard to emulate them. It's only our "fanatical—fortunately marginal—radicals" who claim that the institutional obstacles to individual advancement are *profound*—so profound as to mandate a massive restructuring of our values and our institutions.

I offer my own history as a case in point. I've had what is called an accomplished life—largely because so many people along the way encouraged me to think of myself as "smart" or "gifted." In a less encouraging environment in which all the things I'm *not* good at or *don't* understand had been emphasized, the outcome would have been far different. What, after all, does "smart" mean? That I can add up a series of numbers in my head? I can't. That I can explain Einstein's theory of relativity? I can't. That I can sculpt the human face or design a building? I can't. That I can discuss the intricacies of economic cycles of boom and bust? I can't. Certainly I lack physical prowess; I'm healthy enough, and for my age agile—but could never have played in the NFL or qualified for the U.S. Open. How about "emotional sensitivity"? OK, maybe a touch above average, though I can read other people more easily than I can assign reasons for my own mood swings. Despite all my disqualifications, I was *taught* to ignore them, to stress instead my aptitudes—and was applauded at their every application.

How is it that GLF's radical agenda morphed, more than forty years later, into a movement that stresses above all else the importance of the right to marriage—and, secondarily, to participation on equal terms in killing our country's "enemies"?

In evaluating that shift, we need to make one point abundantly clear at the start: marriage rights did not land on the top of the agenda as the result of a "plot." It wasn't foisted on the LBGTQ majority by a small group of well-placed, privileged gay people; it wasn't the result (as some have claimed) of a few top honchos in certain national organizations—in particular Freedom to Marry and the Human Rights Campaign—somehow tricking or misleading the rest of us into backing the issue. It landed on the top because that's where the majority of gay Americans want it to be; its proven the issue above all others capable of galvanizing the widest support.

From the early days of GLF the left wing of the movement has strongly rejected as mistaken and diversionary the investment of time and resources into a campaign for marriage rights. In the early seventies, traditional—that is, nuclear, monogamous, procreative, male-dominated—marriage was, if anything, a GLF target of scorn, and certainly not an issue it prioritized. By the mid- to late seventies, however, the radical gay movement, which had never represented more than a minority of LGBTQ people, had lost its momentum. In the face of an economic downturn and the country's rightward shift following the end of the war in Southeast Asia, GLF's energy, like that of the larger New Left, drained off into splinter groups, which then scattered. Radical feminism, too, lost its edge. With the rise of "cultural feminism" less was heard about male dominance and sexual freedom and more about women's "closeness to nature" and their opposition to pornography—a depoliticizing process that managed to elide essential differences based on race and class. The culture of resistance was, across the board, turning into a culture of attenuated protest and mounting accommodation.

In the eighties, the advent of AIDS ripped apart and devastated the gay community. Political energy returned in tandem with a refocused target: an indifferent federal government deaf to the swiftly rising death toll and the dire need for help. Where once the gay movement had fought to *remove* hostile government agencies from their lives, it now marshaled its strength in trying to persuade—and then in militantly demanding—that Washington mobilize its immense resources to combat an elusive and terrifying epidemic.

While Washington and the mainstream media twiddled their thumbs—and held their noses—the gay community itself went on a war footing, rallying its own troops—the Gay Men's Health Crisis, the People With AIDS Coalition, ACT UP (AIDS Coalition To Unleash Power)—systematically establishing funding sources and health services, heroically (the claim is not inflated) rising to combat a monstrously formidable enemy in a spirit that "disordered" perverts were thought incapable of manifesting. The toll was terrible: a generation decimated, its survivors despairing. Only belatedly, and then incompletely, did the government respond and new drugs finally emerge that made it possible to take a breath and to begin resumption of something akin to a normal life.

In the gradually reconfigured political landscape of the 1990s, "sexual liberation" no longer widely appealed as a rallying cry. Had not the bathhouses, the rambles, the backroom orgy bars been the very breeding ground of the epidemic? Had not God himself—so the pious, smug legions of the right wing thundered—smitten the sinners? Had not the self-indulgent sexual revolution—a question asked by many gay leaders themselves—gone haywire, mistakenly substituting an endless string of casual, anonymous encounters for the mature comfort of long-term, committed relationships?

It was in this climate that the marriage crusade surfaced and began to pick up steam. Steve Endean's tiny Gay Rights National Lobby, founded in 1980 in Washington, D.C., quickly mushroomed into the renamed Human Rights Campaign Fund (hereafter, HRC—*Fund* was dropped from its title in 1995). HRC proved ready and eager to lead the battered and besmirched gay community out of the wilderness and into the Eden of white picket fences and the miracle of monogamy. Initially, the organization operated as a political action committee focused on raising money to support "worthy" LGB (no *T* yet—no, not for a very long time, and then only under pressure) and gay-friendly candidates for public office. By 1993 HRC had grown exponentially and was far wealthier (and far more conservative) than its nearest rival, the National Gay and Lesbian Task Force. By 1999 HRC boasted a yearly budget of more than 15 million dollars—a Goliath in a land of pigmies. As befitted a mainstream, corporate-like organization, it boasted a board of wealthy, mostly male donors disdainful of any political agenda that even remotely smacked of the revolutionary "nonsense" once spouted by the piddling likes of GLF.

HRC had no use for—and certainly no personal contact with—boisterous screamers like Sylvia Rivera, or a hippie-connected rabble-rouser like Jim Fouratt, who believed not in electoral politics and polite lobbying, but in direct action "zaps," in raucous confrontations with stone-deaf politicians. The new gay politics was bent on respectability, which didn't quite mean a renunciation of "promiscuous" sex but which tacitly removed any discussion of it from the public domain.

It should be added, however, that with the advent of the Trump presidency and the resurgence of antigay legal discrimination (this time in the form of "religious liberty" laws), HRC may have recently turned a progressive corner. In the summer of 2017 it announced plans for investing 26 million dollars in a new grassroots campaign called HRC Rising. The new offshoot will continue to rely on the traditional liberal tools of lobbying and electioneering to defeat anti-LGBTQ legislation and candidates, but it promises as well to focus more on erasing discriminatory practices in the workplace and to operate "in coalition to protect healthcare, defend Planned Parenthood, rally against Trump's Muslim ban, deportation force, and border wall." If HRC follows through on this refurbished agenda, especially in regard to improving the wretched economic plight of working-class gay people, its left-wing critics will, or should, muffle their guns.[4]

In pushing for marriage equality, its advocates didn't seem to be bothered that some 45 percent of heterosexual marriages ended in divorce and another 10 percent in separation. Nor did the fact that the majority of American households consist of unmarried people and that diverse families are now the new American norm. Gays wanted in—wanted to hear, after all the suffering they'd been through, that they were "OK," wanted their unions officially sanctified, wanted public announcements posted on church doors declaring them decent human beings—not obscene sex maniacs—worthy of membership in the great American mainstream. The proponents of marriage claimed that they were fighting for all kinds of families, including those with atypical configurations—though not *too* atypical, it turned out, certainly not what the National Coalition of Gay Organizations had in mind back in 1972 when it had called for "the repeal of all legislative provisions that restrict the sex or number of persons entering into a marriage unit, and [the] extension of legal benefits of marriage to all persons who cohabit regardless of sex or number"—thereby eliminating tax inequities that victimized single people.[5]

From the beginning, the leaders of the gay marriage movement fought for those who looked exactly like the "ideal" straight couple—a two-person monogamous unit. Nontraditional families need not apply—no blended households of spinster siblings or senior citizens, no polyamorous lovers, no adult children serving as caretakers to elderly parents, no extended kinship networks or cross-generational partnerships (or revision of "age of consent" laws)—and certainly no entry for those who'd ever taken up sex work to support themselves, or who championed serial monogamy or group sex. Most important, in terms of sheer numbers alone, no "queer" notions would be entertained about *ending* the assorted privileges that attend state-sanctioned marriage and instead making them available to everyone as universal rights. As the writer-activist Mattilda Bernstein Sycamore plaintively asked, "When did our dreams get so small?"

As the movement for same-sex marriage gathered force, radical objection to its goals gradually began to emerge, with one book in particular helping to bring coherence to the opposition—Michael Warner's 1999 *The Trouble with Normal*. Warner's sophisticated analysis pointed out that LGBTQ couples had already rewritten the standard rules for coupledom; their unions had already proven themselves more egalitarian, more reciprocal in parceling out household chores, and more concerned with ensuring each other's sexual pleasure. Warner further argued that the concept of "false consciousness"—of unwittingly working against one's own best interests—was relevant to the debate over marriage. Proponents of marriage insisted that the concept did not apply, that since gay people overwhelmingly wanted official sanction for their unions, it went against common sense to think that a majority *that* large could be uniformly deceived as to where its advantage lay. Not so, Warner responded. Views that are widely shared often represent not the truth, but rather "the will to naiveté"—false consciousness. "Serfs have revered their masters," he observed," young men have marched gaily off to be slaughtered on behalf of deities and nations, and wives have lovingly obeyed patriarchal husbands."[6]

Marriage advocates countered with the claim that winning the right to marry *was* in the best interest of gay people—they were *not* deceived. Was marriage perfect? Hell no! Was it a better option than disconnected isolation and random sex? Hell yes! Marriage *was* a better way of living than other available options. At its best, as Bishop John Shelby Spong put it, marriage is "marked by integrity and caring and ... filled with grace and beauty."[7] One need not argue, in response to Spong, that he's describing marriage on its best days that few if any real-life versions resemble. One need simply say that advocates of non- or serial monogamy—or, for that matter, of one-night stands—could also generalize from their very best experiences and insist that those instances accurately reflect the whole.

(Camera pans in on a single, superb rose. Voice over: "Isn't this *gorgeous?*" Camera pans out to a dried-up rose bush devoid even of buds.)

A Spong-like defense of marriage implies that it's a more *moral* institution than any of the alternatives. Yet, as Warner puts it, "to presume that morality follows on marriage is to ignore centuries of evidence that each is very much possible without the other." The studies of heterosexual marriage largely agree that it is not good for one's erotic health: sexual attraction to one's mate usually lasts, with luck, about five years; thereafter orgasm generally depends on artificial stimulants like pornography and distancing fantasies about someone—anyone—other than your partner. Those same studies also confirm that in many of those marriages—despite the feminist movement—women still do most of the household chores and child-rearing and in significant numbers still suffer varying forms of domestic violence. If you survive all that, and have a high tolerance for routine, there *is* something to be said for having another eighty-year-old at your side (or on a hospital bed in the next room) as you pass into the twilight zone.

It's sometimes said that heterosexual marriage might be saved, or at least improved, if more gay people joined up and reconfigured the institution in their own image. It *is* true that gay domestic partnerships, based as they usually are on mutuality, might serve as a model and help in humanizing opposite-sex unions. But do we really want to take on that sort of missionary work, knowing as we do that straight men are notoriously resistant to any modification of their privileged role? Wouldn't it be easier and better all around simply to abandon state-sanctioned marriage altogether and offer its menu of privileges—its health care benefits, tax advantages, and the like—to all adults, single or otherwise? Maybe we might then finally realize that intimacy and sexual exclusiveness have no necessary connection.

Katherine Franke, professor of law at Columbia University, has added one other dimension—the most ignored one—to the debate over marriage: not the rights it might bring, but rather the duties, the curtailments on liberty, that it imposes on its practitioners. "In what ways," she asks in her book *Wedlocked*, "are the values, aspirations, and even identity of an oppressed community shaped when they are articulated through the institution of marriage? What kind of freedom and what kind of equality does the capacity to marry mobilize?"[8]

Many gay couples are tying the knot—myself among them—to take advantage of the economic benefits that attend legal marriage. What Franke makes clear is that along with benefits come obligations—*statutory* rules that, if broken, can get you into lots of trouble. The state has now entered into your private relationship, and it will exact its due. The LGBTQ community, Franke warns, is characterized by a variety of family patterns that mainstream Americans deem "unhealthy" or "pathological," and those gay folks not in traditional relationships should prepare themselves for an unpredictable level of contempt and even overt hostility.

Many states, for example, have statutes on the books that criminalize adultery; they've rarely been activated against heterosexuals, but that doesn't mean they won't be against the "lewd and lascivious" behavior (as the "fornication" laws describe it) of certain nontraditional gay relationships. As well, we've already seen the passage in a number of conservative states of "religious freedom restoration acts" designed to excuse discrimination against LGBTQ people on the grounds of "conscience."[9]

It may also surprise some newlyweds to learn that breaking up a marriage is a good deal more difficult than when two partners to a domestic relationship simply decide that "it's no longer working" and improvise the terms of a breakup. It's already true that in some cases of same-sex divorce, "extramarital sex" has been cited as sufficient grounds for denying financial support to the "sinning" partner. Getting a marriage license has given many same-sex couples a sense of "belonging" that they've long craved. Yet a kind of subterfuge has been involved: in practice many same-sex couples ignore the official partnership model of romantic, monogamous love, as do many heterosexual couples, though apparently to a lesser extent. Katherine Franke sums up the situation well: "Gayness has been successfully rebranded by cleaving the sex out of homosexuality"—or pretending to.[10]

She goes one large step further: she raises doubts as to whether the bargain has been worth the candle. Alternative forms of attachment like nonmonogamous partnerships or group intimacy may not go by the wayside, but neither are they likely to be openly championed as preferable to the nuclear family. What has been most innovative about the erotic patterns that have evolved over time in the gay community may partly be abandoned or wholly concealed—or we will otherwise run the serious risk of being rebranded as unredeemable renegades incapable of changing our "bizarre" behavior.

We've come full circle, back some fifty years to the debate that consumed GLF and set it apart from groups that followed, such as the Gay Activists Alliance: Where do we want to place the emphasis—on liberty or on equality? GLF emphasized sexual and emotional liberation, as a necessary prelude, not a substitute, for creating an egalitarian society. GAA put the focus on winning equal access to all the rights of citizenship; its tactical "zaps" may have been radically confrontational, but "respect"—

not a reconfigured society—was its primary goal. GLF birthed the trans movement; GAA was godfather to the drive for marriage equality.

The gay left has all along rejected the campaign for traditional marriage as misguided—intrinsically mistaken as well as diversionary: mistaken because all the privileges marriage confers should, by rights, be extended automatically to *all* our citizens; diversionary because it has contributed to the gay movement's failure to understand that most gay Americans are *working-class*—and that's true whether class is defined by income, job status, or educational level. The chief issues for working-class gay people these days relate not to whether they're deemed "eligible" for state-sanctioned wedding bells, but rather to matters concerning health care, homelessness, deportation, lack of full-time employment, low pay, and violence in the workplace. Finding a job with decent wages and keeping that job (since in half the states employers can still fire workers simply because they're gay) are *more* difficult than was once true. When they do find work, many gay people, like too many other Americans, are employed at monotonous, soul-destroying labor, and given little or no sick leave, paid vacations, benefits—or respect. On top of that, they live in fear of being laid off; today only 11 percent of American workers belong to a union, which means they lack any collective power to force contract negotiations on an employer. And some prominent union activists—among them, Andy Stern, the former president of Service Employees International Union (SEIU; one of the country's largest), there is serious doubt, given automation, employer hostility, and overseas competition, whether unions even *have* a future, let alone a powerful one.[11]

In some gay-friendly white-collar unions like SEIU, whose membership includes many women and people of color, the tolerance level for LGBTQ workers is high, and most of them have "come out" without serious repercussions. Still, the Williams Institute on Sexual Orientation Law and Public Policy has found that in the workforce as a whole, roughly a quarter of gay workers have experienced some form of discrimination on the job—and a whopping 90 percent of transgender workers— including being fired or passed over for promotion and being verbally or physically abused. Yet Congress has refused to pass the Employment Non-discrimination Act (ENDA) (itself a disputed "benefit") to outlaw workplace discrimination based on gender identity or sexual orientation.

In many blue-collar jobs, unions are weak or nonexistent, the mostly male workforce is pronouncedly homophobic, and the workplace poses a constant danger for many gay workers. Anne Balay, in her pioneering study *Steel Closets,* has given us a detailed ethnography of what daily life is like for LGBTQ blue-collar workers in northwestern Indiana at one of the steel industry's few remaining plants. (The days of John L. Lewis and a thriving union, the Steel Workers Organizing Committee (SWOC), are long gone. Steel employed 650,000 Americans in the early 1950s; today that figure has dwindled to 150,000.) In the world of the steel mills, Balay writes, "gay people are profoundly invisible, ... isolated and scared," and an old-school macho culture still reigns supreme. Facing stiff competition from more modern mills elsewhere in the world, "many union stewards ... fear rocking the boat, especially when an issue does not affect the majority" of workers. The union stays focused on matters relating to mill safety and salaries—if anything, Balay reports, it's "a party to the harassment and silencing" of queer workers.[12]

Balay makes a powerful case for the profound difficulties of gay working-class life, describing her informants as "bitter, exhausted, devalued, and at risk." The shift to a more accepting attitude toward gay people in the culture at large has found limited echo in the world of blue-collar workers. For gay steelworkers, Balay writes, "the world has gotten less rather than more accepting"—perhaps because paternalistic family life is still strong and blue-collar males tend to view any threat to gender role conformity as a direct assault on their authority.

What does the middle-class gay movement know or care about the dangers and dirty jobs characteristic of hot blast furnaces and fearsome walkways? Not a thing. Nor, for that matter, does the national movement seem to care about the different but still-wretched conditions that attend minimum wage, part-time service jobs. The most prominent and prosperous gay organizations—the Human Rights Campaign (HRC) and the National LGBTQ Task Force—seem astonishingly unaware (or unconcerned) that the majority of LGBTQ people *are* working-class. Balay's steelworkers are entirely off these organization's radar; they might as well be natives of Croatia for all the attention they get from the national movement; the blue-collar working class is a foreign culture, speaking an undecipherable language (and it isn't queer theory).

In rebuttal, a typical HRC or Task Force member might say, defensively, "Well, as far as steelworkers go, they *do* get paid well, right?" Yes, they do—and they're also prone to debilitating disease and early death (few steelworkers live beyond sixty-five). On top of that, those among them who are gay either silently endure mistreatment on the mill floor—or quit. Usually they choose silence (they do have to eat). They also choose, understandably, to identify with class rather than with sexual orientation issues.

Queer steelworkers have no other place to go, since their unions are focused on workplace issues. Hiding their private lives (or trying to—though some few do choose to come out), and maintaining constant vigilance against discovery and the bigotry, harassment, and violence that usually follow, produces a high level of daily stress and anxiety—and alcoholism.

Back in 1970, GLF as a group never sought an alliance with organized labor, in part because the trade union movement—so powerful in the 1930s—had already lost its militant edge. Once-radical unions turned bureaucratic and centrist as early as the 1950s, and racial divisions within the working class became more pronounced than the socialist vision of labor solidarity. Not only was class conflict in 1970 off the table, but racial conflict was prominently on it. GLF sought what few allies were available in the left wing of the civil rights movement and among radical feminists.

Besides, organized labor harbored a backlog of animosity between its straight rank and file and the young radicals of various stripes who'd been taking to the streets to protest various forms of injustice. In the sixties, antiwar protest had held center stage, and the animosity between the student radicals of SDS (Students for a Democratic Society) and the patriotic hardhats of the labor movement became so pronounced that SDS's famous founding document, the Port Huron Statement, actually faulted the union movement for its "accommodation and limited effectiveness." A small number of radical lesbians and gay men—Judy Grahn and Leslie Feinberg were the best known—did join the Workers World party (Feinberg became managing editor of the party's newspaper), a breakaway splinter group from the Socialist Workers Party, but affiliation for most of them was tentative and brief.[13]

Most of the young radicals of GLF ignored class-related issues; to the extent they'd heard about earlier struggles for economic justice, they tended to shrug at what they viewed as a lost cause that had yielded few benefits for the working class—and had in any case been superseded (in their eyes) by a cultural revolution that centered on issues relating to gender and sexuality. As I myself wrote in 1973, the socialist goal of

> man free from material want" had given way to the search for "a new utopia in the area of psychosexual transformation ... a gender revolution in which 'male' and 'female' have become outmoded differentiations, individual human beings instead combining in their persons the qualities previously thought the preserve of one gender or the other. It's possible to argue that this new vision— when most of the world still goes to bed hungry at night—is a luxury and an illusion, the decadent yearning of that portion of society already sated with possessions but not with the satisfaction they were supposed to have brought in train.[14]

As I saw it, the radical young, with more than a touch of arrogance, disdained any interest in a Marxist paradigm that saw changes in material relationships as the necessary prelude to changes in cultural patterns.

Most GLFers had been brought up with a middle-class mindset (though some were not middle-class) characterized by optimism and high expectations. Though many of them had no jobs or only fly-by-night ones and, by any economic standard, would have been considered downwardly mobile, few had been *born* into poverty. They lacked the kind of silent resignation that often accompanies a generational history of penury—the weary certainty that protesting one's lot in life is futile.

That kind of long-suffering forbearance was utterly foreign to most GLFers. Their attitude lined up more closely—though with a difference—with the values of the anarchistic counter-culture and with the politics of SDS. Like the counterculture, many in GLF challenged traditional gender and sexual norms; like most of the activist young who joined the ranks of SDS, they shared the middle-class conviction that the squeaky wheel gets oiled—*if* one squeaks loud enough. GLF was far more overtly political than the hippies, and far less sexist than the males in SDS. They rejected equally the counterculture's apo-litical "turn on, tune out" attitude and the macho aggressiveness of the white New Left and the Black Panthers. The radical young men and lesbians who joined GLF took their cues instead from feminism—or at least many of the men tried to, though their good intentions often fell short.

Only a small subset from the middle class (or any class), of course, ever becomes active in left-wing protest. The vast major-ity—as the current agenda of the gay movement testifies—focus not on attacking established values and institutions, but on saluting them. Why a *few* do not remains one of the many mys-teries, the answer to which probably lies somewhere in the deep recesses of toddler psychology. What we do know is that the great majority of middle-class, white, college-educated men (and quite a few women) want to win their stripes in the society *as it is,* and that such discontent as they might sometimes feel with "the system" is further circumscribed by their assurance that the incidental social inequities they do acknowledge will in due course be self-corrective.

Most people, quite simply, want to belong. Life's daily strug-gles—yes, even for the middle class—consume the bulk of one's time and sap most of one's energy, with the rest of it consumed by the gnawing sense, which not even the busiest of lives can entirely blot out, that life is going to end, and in all likelihood painfully. In the brief interlude preceding, we need all the comfort we can get, and that includes for most of us the comfort of being certified and approved—accepted as a human being in good standing. It should therefore come as no surprise that most gay people, too, yearn to fit in, to belong, and to that end are happy to pledge allegiance to whatever the going institutional structure is and whatever official formula for happiness reigns—which in our culture is still (though it's wobbling) lifetime monogamous pair-bonding. Most of us also associate legal marriage with respectability and security. We strive to have our relationships mimic as closely as possible those of the straight majority—even as heterosexuals, ironically, are in ever-increasing numbers defecting from traditional marriage and binding monogamy.[15]

In the years immediately following the Stonewall riots, the overwhelming majority of gay people remained closeted, their energy focused on avoiding detection and disgrace. Only a comparative handful joined GLF, gave voice to heretical views, or denounced what the majority accepted: racism, sexism, imperialism, and capitalism. Their words could be vacuous, their solutions confused and utopian. Yet their search for plausible, satisfying ways to live deserves respect. And even gratitude—for their insistence that injustice be named and opposed. Unlike most of their youthful contemporaries, who hid their nonconformities and sought to "get along," those who joined GLF blatantly paraded their "differentness" and their dissent—in the process forcing a confrontation about their larger legitimacy. A small, vocal group, out of all proportion to its numbers, often sets a generation's political agenda, plants the seeds for more consequential efforts to come. These fresh, fiery voices were at the time the most loudly vocal ones in the gay community—and taken as typifying a new generation of uncompromising, hell-raising queers.

GLF chapters did in fact spring up in a dozen other cities in the United States (and in London, whose chapter was especially active); they rarely mobilized more than a few dozen people, but they were no less radical than the GLF voices sounded in New York. In some of the chapters (not New York's) the burning—and most controversial—question related to age-of-consent laws.

In approaching that issue, I start with a simple question: Did you have sex before you were sixteen? You did? Was the other person (or persons) of the same or opposite gender? (Yes, I know: the phrasing suggests the outmoded notion of fixed genders, but "same or opposite" remains the language of the courts. And the courts are at the heart of my question.) Almost all states have laws on their books that establish the legal age of sexual consent at sixteen. That, purportedly, is the age at which—to quote one of the statutes—teenagers reach "cognitive maturity" and become "rational decision makers." No, they still can't legally buy a beer, vote, or get married—though they can drive a car. Go figure.

Before engaging more closely with the thorny question, What is the appropriate age at which "sexual consent" can be said to exist? let me be as blindingly clear as I can that I do not discount to any degree the horrendous amount of abuse, rape, and trauma that accompanies the sexual coming-of-age in this (and I suspect every) country. Stories of brutal molestation and its awful life-long consequences are, alas, a scourge across the land. They're not, of course, confined to teenagers—children as young as two and people of advanced age have also been its victims—and sexual exploitation frequently leaves its survivors with scars that never heal and psychic pain of profound intensity.

Three quite separate issues are at stake here: adults having sex with prepubescent children; adults having sex with postpubescent teenagers; and teenagers having sex with each other. As for the first of these—adult molestation of prepubescent children—there can surely be no rational or moral dissent from the view that the law must be sweeping, airtight, and vigorously enforced. And it must be acknowledged more than it usually is that in most cases involving the sexual abuse of minors, family members and adult family friends—or clergy—are the perpetrators.[16]

As for teenagers having sex with each other, the current consensus among the experts (not to be confused with the teenagers) is that age sixteen somehow marks the magical moment when sexual readiness becomes manifest. That consensus is well established but far from impregnable. Several problems with it immediately arise. For starters, the fixed rigidity of sixteen ignores the dissimilar timetables at which individuals reach puberty—that point at which the body announces its physical preparedness and the mind has trouble focusing on anything *other* than sex. For many youngsters, that point is reached well before the age of sixteen. At summer camp I and my prepubescent bunk mates (age ten? twelve?) used to regularly derive pleasure from lying down and rubbing up against each other— "fussing" we called it. Were we "having sex," or is orgasm a prerequisite? That our pleasure was guilt-ridden—we "fussed" in secret, beyond the gaze of the counselors—probably does qualify the activity (in our still-puritanical culture) as sexual.

The current consensus that sets sixteen as the appropriate age for sexual consent implies agreement that "adulthood" has at that point been reached, though many other rights of citizenship—like voting—are still denied. Even in regard to sex, setting the legal age at sixteen fails to match up either to historical or to cross-cultural practice. Until the late nineteenth century, the legal age of sexual consent—even in the United States—was everywhere lower than today. The first known law about the matter was passed in England in 1275, making it illegal to "ravish" a maiden under the age of twelve (lowered to ten in 1576) without her consent; until the start of the nineteenth century it remained legal in England to have sex with a ten-year-old girl.

Lest we puff up with pride at our superior morality, in the state of Delaware *until the mid-1960s* a middle-aged man could legally have sexual intercourse with a seven-year-old girl *or* boy. In fact the very concept of adolescence began to emerge only in the last quarter of the nineteenth century; before that, children were regarded as having achieved adulthood at the onset of puberty. As for marriage, before about 1850, it was thought entirely ordinary for girls to marry (or, more accurately, to be married off) at ten, sometimes as young as seven, though the marriage, in most cases, wasn't consummated until the onset of puberty.

The presence or absence of the young girl's "informed consent" was not, it seems, a consideration. Neither girls nor grown women were generally regarded as capable of active agency; their volition, or lack thereof, was an irrelevance. As for boys, they've historically been seen as maturing later than girls, and less in need of protection. Where male homosexual acts were involved, the argument developed that the social consequences of such behavior were dire and that the needed age of consent should therefore be set higher.

Ah "consent." Therein of course lies the heart of contention: how to recognize and define that moment in the life cycle when an individual can be confidently said to be a free agent capable of a fully conscious and volitional response to a sexual overture. Not being a philosopher, or even a psychiatrist, I'll have to leave aside the endlessly debated conundrum of whether one is *ever* entirely or even partly a "free agent" (rather than a robotic responder)—whether at sixteen, forty, or eighty—to a given aggregate of stimuli. It might be worth adding that in the instance of religious indoctrination no one seems concerned about the morality of indoctrinating young children to believe in and serve a supernatural being—though they lack the "cognitive capacity" to "consent" to such brainwashing.

For an answer to the puzzle of when (and whether) free agency can be said to be present, many turn for answers to "science"—and (if they're like me) soon turn disgruntledly away from its fog-shrouded contradictions. On the matter of consent, "science" is not the equivalent of value-free certitude. Some scientists insist that *no* teenager is capable of fully rational decision making, sexual or otherwise: the human brain, they confidently assert, continues to mature throughout the teen years. Using terminology like "neural plasticity" and "epigenetics" designed to reduce us to quivering yeah-sayers, the scientists place special emphasis on the all-important prefrontal cortex. Citing—I kid you not—Shimamura's Dynamic Filtering Theory, they claim that during the teen years the prefrontal cortex hasn't yet mustered its full "executive power" to inhibit impulsive, inappropriate behavior, to rein in the need to express intense emotion (like sexual desire), and to allow for the delaying of gratification and the weighing of consequences.

Unfortunately, brain imaging is still in its infancy, and we know far too little about its functional components to confidently link, say, a specific developmental marker to a particular behavioral trait, such as logical reasoning. Even if we were to grant that everyone's prefrontal cortex does indeed control all the behaviors currently assigned it, we'd still be left with the inconvenient fact that not all brains mature at the same rate. As with our other body parts, maturation varies widely among individuals. Some girls start to menstruate at ten or eleven, others not till fifteen. Perhaps those who reach puberty early are also ahead of the pack in developing mature prefrontal cortexes. Or maybe—the question *has* been raised—there's no such thing as a "mature" brain; maybe from birth to death it continues to change and evolve as it interacts with continuously shifting environmental stimuli, the timetable and efficacy peculiar to each individual.

Anyway, we don't look through a microscope when judging a person's maturity; we base our assessment on the person's observed behavior. Though we observers may be convinced that our judgment issues from a timeless ethical standard, that can only mean we know little history and less anthropology; in fact, different cultures through time have varied widely in their definitions of "normal" or "appropriate" sexuality. Globally, some seventy-five or eighty countries impose sanctions of various kinds against same-sex intimacy—and in five the punishment is death. In the Caribbean, Jamaica mandates ten years at hard labor for homosexual acts, yet Cuba—whose concentration camps for gay people back in 1970 infuriated Allen Young and other young radicals in the Gay Liberation Front—now has, according to Maurice Tomlinson, "the most extensive protections" for gay people in the northern Caribbean.[17]

Variations in the rest of the world are no less pronounced. In regard to Africa, many nationalists once claimed (evidence to the contrary now abounds) that homosexuality had been unknown until brought to the continent by the colonial powers. Today Uganda continues to harbor widespread antigay violence, while South Africa has passed progressive antidiscrimination laws. India has a long history of respecting "gender queer" people, yet in 2014 its Supreme Court recriminalized homosexuality. And so it goes, the variations in attitude and legality covering the spectrum.

It can perhaps safely be said, in regard to the "age of consent" issue, that on average eighteen-year-olds have more information and experience than thirteen-year-olds, but even that presumed truism is open to debate: Have the eighteen-year-olds been fed *reliable* information? Have they been subject to the kind of positive experience that leads to honesty and integrity?

What we do know for certain is that at least a third of today's teens under sixteen *are* already having sex; they're listening to their bodies, not to their parents, priests—or scientists. In a recent CDC Youth Risk Survey, roughly two-thirds of high school students acknowledged having sex before graduation—and despite potentially severe legal consequences. If an overzealous police officer raids the local lovers' lane and arrests two minors for having sex with each other—or sometimes just for touching or kissing—their names will likely be entered on the state's sex offender registry. And once on a sex offender registry, you stay on—currently the public and searchable rolls contain nearly 800,000 names, some of them people as young as fourteen—and the consequences are devastating in terms of being unable to find jobs, shelter, companionship—or staying out of jail. According to Judith Levine, a quarter of convicted "sex offenders" are minors, eleven to seventeen years old.[18]

"Sex offender" and "queer" have long been linked in the popular mind, yet the mainstream gay organizations have barely raised a peep about either the linkage or the incarceration that follows. Criminal justice issues *are* prominent in the agendas of the radical gay organizations that have been forming recently on the local level, but the Human Rights Campaign seems unable to recognize illegitimate incarceration as part of a civil rights–based agenda—not even when the arbitrary injustice is palpable. North Carolina state law, to give but one example, permits two sixteen-year-olds to have sex, but if they take pictures, they're subject to being charged with a felony.

Why the blindness—or is it indifference?—to the severe consequences that descend on minors caught having sex with each other? Isn't it perfectly natural that fourteen-year-olds want to explore their sexuality—that such experimentation isn't a crime or a sin? After all, Freud revealed (in *Three Essays*) that children much younger than fourteen are curious about their bodies, engage in sex play, and masturbate. The real crime is to tell ourselves that we're "protecting" the young; they do need protection—from "sexual predators" but not usually from themselves or one another. What we're protecting when we interfere with and condemn youthful experimentation is our own excessively priggish selves. To punish sexual experimentation in the young is the surest way to turn out yet another generation of guilt-ridden prudes, of adults who associate sex with shame and filth.

In other countries today, the age of consent is lower than sixteen—it's fourteen in Germany, Portugal, and Italy (and, yes, the Vatican!); fifteen in France and Poland. Teenage pregnancy rates are also lower than in the United States, probably because those same countries encourage the kind of sex education in the schools that includes detailed discussion of contraception, STDs, and condoms, and teaches good "refusal" skills. Instead of criminalizing sex between teenagers under sixteen (in a few states the age of consent has been pushed up to eighteen), we need to focus on equipping teenagers with enough information to defend themselves against disease, pregnancy, and middle-aged predators; well-informed youngsters are the best protection against unwanted sexual advances. We also need to pass stringent laws against indecent assault, coercive sex, and rape.

In discussing all these matters, the word *pedophilia* is thrown around a good deal, often with a remarkable lack of precision. The term should be rigorously confined to adult seduction of prepubescent youth—which is overwhelmingly a heterosexual phenomenon that usually takes place within families and is always wrong (though sex play between very young children themselves is a different matter—it's natural and inevitable). Unfortunately the term *pedophilia* is often used to describe (and denounce) sex between *post*pubescent youth between the ages of twelve and eighteen and someone older. Where sex between two postpubescent teenagers need not—as I've been arguing— be viewed as problematic, once we introduce a partner age eighteen or older into the equation, the issue becomes trickier.

Why aren't we talking more about all this? Why aren't sexual rights being championed (when mentioned at all) with anything like the enthusiasm with which we defend "human" rights? Why isn't freedom of sexual expression just as important a "rights" issue as, say, freedom of speech? Why—since the matters at hand relate at least as much to gay as to straight youth—aren't the national gay organizations doing more—doing much of *anything*—to engage with gay teenagers, some of whom have been thrown out of their houses and are in urgent need of comfort and support? The national gay movement today does pay some heed to the unique needs of gay youth, mostly to their high incidence of homelessness (estimated even in liberal San Francisco at 30 to 35 percent), but the glance has too often been sideways and reluctant, as if having been unwillingly distracted from more pressing matters (like marriage and military rights).

Though guidance counseling on college campuses has gotten less squeamish in regard to gay sexuality, it can sometimes still be destructive. One 2016 lawsuit illustrates the point. Andrew Cash, a counselor at Missouri State University was fired from his job when, citing his "religious beliefs," he refused to counsel gay couples. Describing himself as "a Christian with sincerely-held beliefs" (in contrast to Christians who hold insincere beliefs?), Cash sued the university, and at this writing, the case is still pending. His lawyer has proudly informed the media that in his view "Christians have to go on the offensive, or it's going to be a situation like Sodom and Gomorrah in the Bible, where you aren't safe to have a guest in your home, with the demands of the gay mob." (Who mentioned a mob? Honestly, some straight men's fantasies!)

The culture in general has grown more accepting of LGBTQ people in recent years, but for many gay teens, high-school remains a living hell. In 2016 the Centers for Disease Control released the results of an in-depth study of more than 15,000 gay, lesbian, and bisexual students in grades 9 through 12 (trans or "gender-fluid" teens were not included). What the survey revealed is that acceptance remains patchy and partial. LGB students are nearly three times as likely as heterosexual students to skip school out of fear for their safety, are forced four times more often than their straight counterparts "to have unwanted sex," and are roughly five times as likely to have attempted suicide in the past twelve months.[19]

These days it's more acceptable in our high schools (sometimes even "cool") to be different—but not *too* different. Transgender teens do draw allies in the more progressive high schools, but they run a daily gauntlet elsewhere. In the United States as a whole, Protestant fundamentalism is alive and well, and apparently as fiercely trans- and homophobic as ever. What the high schools (as well as college campuses like Missouri State) need is an upgrade in sexual "health and hygiene" courses that includes some history and anthropology—some awareness of how, across time and cultures, "normal" sexuality has been socially defined in a mind-opening variety of ways: Something along the lines, say, of discussing the Berbers of Egypt's Siwa Oasis, whose sexual habits stunned one visiting anthropologist as far back as 1937. "All normal Siwan men and boys practice sodomy," the anthropologist wrote in consternation; "the natives are not ashamed of this; they talk about it as openly as they talk about love of women."[20]

Some fifty years ago, during GLF's brief life, the range of inquiry wasn't nearly as narrow as it is now. The gay liberation movement held far more radical views and more encompassing interests regarding teenage sexuality than do today's national LGBTQ organizations. The tone was sharper and the range of issues broader. Radical voices are still heard today, but they emanate primarily from queer public intellectuals, mostly based in the universities, and from emerging gay organizations on the local level—groups like SONG (Southerners on New Ground), based in Atlanta.

During GLF's heyday any number of crusty orthodoxies relating to sexuality came on the chopping block, and questions relating to the age of consent remained high on GLF's agenda. Even as late as 1976, after the forces of gay assimilationism had pretty much routed the firebrands and seized control of the movement, the Canadian writer Gerald Hannon published a piece in Toronto's radical gay magazine, the *Body Politic,* that debunked the "archaic" notion of the innocent child disinterested in sex and immune to its pleasures. In the body of his essay Hannon makes clear that he defines the children he's talking about as post-, not prepubescent teenagers—though (mistakenly) he doesn't explicitly say so.[21]

Hannon argues that most adults link sex with "the most explosive human passions" and thus conclude that a youngster is "simply incapable of surviving such a situation"—they're "too innocent ... too defenseless." (As I argue earlier, many teenagers in today's "hookup culture" *don't* tend to link sex with "the debilitating passions of the heart.") In any case, Hannon champions youthful sexual exploration not simply because it's "natural" and provides pleasure, but also because sex "is a centrifugal force which leads one outward into the community," helping young people to discover sooner rather than later that—another radical notion no longer of much interest to the mainstream gay movement—"your family is not necessarily the only locus of human warmth and affection." Hannon then dots the *i:* "Happiness," he writes, "could be something other than living with one other person ... for the rest of one's life." Directly attacking the presumed sanctity of traditional family life, Hannon reminds us that it was (and to a large measure still is) based on "the unpaid labor of one person—the woman—to guarantee the continuance of the underpaid labor of another—the man."

Views comparable to Hannon's on sex, monogamy, and the family were often sounded during the early days of the gay movement—and at a time when "sodomy" was defined as a crime in all but two states, when gay couples holding hands in public were arrested for "lewd" or "disorderly" conduct, and when police raids on gay bars and cruising spots were commonplace. These were also the years when respected psychiatrists (Lawrence Hatterer and Lionel Ovesey are prime examples) were all but unanimous in equating homosexuality with illness. They did so contra Freud, who viewed "constitutional bisexuality as characteristic of all

human beings" and argued that even in a pronouncedly homophobic culture it remained possible "to point to some trace or
other of a homosexual object choice in everyone." Throughout
the sixties the psychiatric profession as a whole held to the view
that homosexual behavior was the mark of a disturbed, pathological personality—a view exemplified in psychiatrist David
Reuben's huge best seller, *Everything You Always Wanted to Know
about Sex but Were Afraid to Ask,* in which he flatly declared the
impossibility of any homosexual leading a contented life.

It wasn't just psychiatry. In a 1970 essay in *Harper's,* the highly
regarded critic Joseph Epstein echoed the view of many straight
intellectuals that homosexuality was "a curse." Nothing his sons
could do would make him more ashamed, Epstein wrote, than
"if any of them were to become homosexual." If possible, he continued—in genocidal language reminiscent of Nazi Germany
(remarkably, Epstein was Jewish)—he would "wish homosexuality off the face of the earth."[22]

Any number of other well-known liberals—including Adam
Walinsky, the former aide to Robert Kennedy, and Nicolas von
Hoffman, a much-admired journalist who'd earlier been a field
organizer for Saul Alinsky—added their denunciatory voices, at
best mocking, at worst defamatory. The black radical Eldridge
Cleaver, whose scalding *Soul on Ice* justly excoriated the brutal
treatment of blacks, had no trouble raining down bigoted scorn
on gay people: "Homosexuality is a sickness, just as are rape or
wanting to become head of General Motors."

It took courage in those years just to "come out," let alone to
publish radical views—as Hannon's arrest and trial attest.
"Courage" of course, is something of an arbitrary signifier; other
observers—and not merely conservatives—substituted less flat-
tering terminology, including "foolhardy," "irresponsible," and

"stupid." Yet the early liberationists were remarkably undaunted. They even paid back Cleaver's scorn with open and strenuous support for the Panthers and Young Lords.

Then, within a few short years, it was all over. The tiny number of blacks and Latinos in GLF soon decamped to new radical formations for people of color, like Third World Gay Revolution. The lesbian minority in GLF concluded that their gay male "brothers" were incapable of treating them as more than distant cousins; even those of goodwill proved more comfortable being around men than women. A sizable group of "liberal"—as opposed to "radical"—gay men decided, after all, that they preferred representative to pure democracy, Robert's Rules to creative anarchism, and equal rights in "things as they are" rather than working toward "things as they might be." In 1973 they formed the National Gay Task Force—only belatedly adding the word "Lesbian"—and set out to lobby for an end to discrimination (rather than an end to injustice).

The remnants of GLF gave up the ghost and scattered to the four corners. The walls of Jericho had not come down, a result that many, back in 1969, seem actually to have expected. At the end, there were inevitable recriminations about one another's failings of understanding or friendship. What had started out as an angry determination to end the pathologizing of gay people ended in arcane debates and debilitating complaints about trivial slights and grievances. What collapsed was not Jericho, but GLF.

And yet ... GLF had aimed high. It had tackled issues much broader—such as internalized sexism and racism—than the gay agenda that replaced GLF, an agenda limited (as I would later describe it) to "getting sodomy statues off the books, or putting anti-discrimination laws on them." Goals well worth achieving, though not exactly, taken together, visionary. GLF, for all its shortcomings, had never confused winning legislative and legal battles with the ultimate goals of the movement. GLF wanted more than incorporation into the status quo—more for the country as a whole, not just for gay people. It hoped to raise consciousness nationwide about ingrained American racism and imperialism, and it challenged as well a national mindset that equated heterosexuality with normalcy, the nuclear family with optimal human happiness, and dichotomous gender roles with divine intention. GLF's life was short, but its legacy long—and deep.

III

Equality or Liberation?

In his book *It's Not Over* (2015), Michelangelo Signorile convincingly argues that "victory blindness" has encouraged us to minimize the many obstacles that remain in the path of first-class citizenship for gay people. Homophobia is in fact alive and well. The surge in "acceptance" has been paralleled by a rise in hostility. Even the liberal metropolis of New York City saw a 27 percent spike in antigay violence from 2013 to 2014. LGBTQ teenagers, a small minority of all teens, still account for roughly one-third of teen suicides. An increasing number of Republican lawmakers have turned to the so-called religious defense to protect business owners refusing service to LGBTQ customers. And "acceptance" on the part of straights is in many cases, as considerable evidence shows, predicated on the widely held assumption that homosexual desire is hardwired—a view based on flawed research (which I discuss in this chapter).[1]

Backlash is a familiar phenomenon that has always attended movements for social justice. Many Americans who self-describe as liberal, and who in recent decades have increasingly come to accept gay people as neither sick nor sinful, often base that acceptance on an unexpressed, and unexamined set of premises: "We take you at your word: you *are* like us; now that we've 'let you in,' we expect that in your gratitude you won't pull any surprises and start behaving like some subspecies that you've assured us you're not; if we now say it's OK to be gay, we don't expect you to pull the rug out from under us and start acting *queer.*" This is the political bargain known as assimilation: agree to act "normal"—as *the mainstream* defines normalcy.

Kenji Yoshino, professor of law at Yale, in his nuanced book *Covering: The Hidden Assault on Our Civil Rights* (2006), persuasively argues that we all assimilate to some degree, that the process is a "precondition of civilization—to speak a language, to curb violent urges, and to obey the law are all acts of assimilation. Through such acts we rise above the narrow stations of our lives to enter into a broader mindfulness, and often, paradoxically, we must do this to elaborate ourselves as individuals." Yoshino goes on to argue *against* "coerced assimilation not supported by reasons—against a reflexive conformity that takes itself as its own rationale." He then proceeds for the remainder of his valuable book to discuss "illegitimate" reasons—ones based on "simple animus" that assumes "one group is ... less worthy than another"—for demanding that "gays assimilate to straight norms, or that women assimilate to male norms, or that racial minorities assimilate to white norms."[2]

As a legal scholar, Yoshino has discovered that in case after case a gay individual who "covers"—that is, downplays "stigmatized attributes" like male effeminacy—fares far better in the courts (indeed, in life in general) than one who does not. Individuals whose homosexuality is "discreetly" (though openly) displayed win their discrimination or custody cases far more often than those who behave in court "flamboyantly." What has also become clear to him is that affectionate acts like hugging or kissing that are treated as normal in a heterosexual couple are regarded as "inappropriate behavior" in a gay one. Such "flagrancy" is often treated as "dangerous" in front of children whose gender and sexual identities are not yet formed. The courts also regard being politically active as suspect. According to Yoshino, many gays are not only complicit in "covering" but "do not view covering—even when coerced—as a harm to personhood."

The courts react similarly in regard to race: a black person able to prove that skin color was the reason for having been fired will win in court, but that same person will lose if fired for sporting a braided hairstyle. As Yoshino puts it, "immutable" aspects of racial identity are protected; "mutable" ones are not. Women, too, are subject to the double bind: they must appear "masculine" enough to do the job, but not so masculine as to threaten the gender binary. Historically the assimilationist vision of the United States as a "melting pot" has never comported closely with the reality of ghettoized lives—yet the view that it does has recently returned with force. Rationality, in short supply, has never been the handmaiden of prejudice. Nor can the *reality* of pluralism convince anyone of its necessity.

Like Yoshino, Signorile believes it's utterly premature to talk about the "victory" of the gay freedom struggle, and, in *It's Not Over,* he lays out his many reasons, focusing primarily on citing examples which show that gay people have yet to reach the promised land of first-class citizenship. Signorile is less interested than Yoshino in exploring the internal accommodations gay people continue to make in order to win acceptance as "normal"—and the impediment that accommodation creates to the achievement of liberation. Yoshino's uneasiness about the costs of assimilation echo in more nuanced form the concerns that profoundly troubled GLF radicals back in 1970, whereas Signorile's focus is on winning (in his words) "the battle for full equality"—equality, not liberation—which recalls the more modulated politics of GAA and the National Gay Task Force, the organizations that followed GLF.

Signorile admires and quotes from Yoshino. He's also at pains to emphasize one particular point of agreement: many gay people who appear "average" and behave in "mainstream" ways—enjoying football, joining the military, raising children, playing the lottery—are *not* "covering." They *authentically* prefer the mainstream lifestyle (that is, to the extent any of us can authentically evaluate and consciously choose to behave this way and not that).

It hardly needs saying that Signorile isn't wrong in wanting an end to discrimination based on sexual orientation in housing, employment, education, health, and public accommodations. These are real issues demanding continuing attention; the demand for first-class citizenship must be ongoing and relentless. The central question, rather, is how we present ourselves to the mainstream when making our demands. Is it in fact accurate to describe ourselves as "just folks"? When making that claim, are we disguising or disavowing the many ways in which we do in fact stand culturally apart from the mainstream—*essential* ways, of value not only to ourselves but also potentially to the mainstream?

So far as I'm aware, none of us on the Left would ever want to argue, or even imply, that we don't want equal access to all of society's rights and opportunities. We're against any and all forms of discrimination whether based on sexual orientation or on race, gender, ethnicity, religious faith, IQ, HIV status, able-bodiedness—or all-around queerness. We want legislation passed to ensure all of that—and we want it enforced. Don't trust polls, Signorile valuably warns us, that show a steady and sizable shrinkage in prejudice. There *has* been some reduction—and in regard to race and gender, as well as sexual orientation.

But what people tell pollsters is often at odds what they privately feel. They may no longer call you a "nigger" in public, but that doesn't mean they *feel* you're their equal or that you're fully entitled to their respect. The climate of opinion has shifted *enough* to make bigots realize that the mainstream now frowns on outright intolerance—or at least its public expression. Millennials are unquestionably more tolerant, even more appreciative, of diversity than their elders, but the field has hardly been swept clean of haters—though they've learned how to substitute coded bias for explicit bigotry. Besides, the unrepentant elders continue to run the show. In some states, as Signorile carefully documents, it's still legal for restaurant owners to refuse service to gay (or gay-appearing) people, for landlords to deny them a lease, and for employers to fire (or never hire) them. For trans people, it's all worse—a good deal worse.

Besides, prejudice is not monolithic. Recent studies have shown that although a majority now favors civil rights for gays and lesbians, "informal forms of sexual prejudice"—like disapproving public displays of affection—remain strong. Put in everyday terms, you can legally marry now, but you risk harassment and even violence if you smooch while walking down the street. Heterosexual men feel a good deal more threatened than do heterosexual women at the sight of two men kissing—even if it's on the cheek. Two women kissing are less at risk, since the culture is far more permissive about females—those emotional creatures—displaying tenderness or affection.[3]

How to handle the angry heterosexual male? That's tricky. Fighting back against bullies is a physically dangerous business. And the tactic of friendly humor doesn't seem to work any better. Those gay men who refuse to curtail their affection for each other in public are admirably asserting their right to be themselves— but unpleasant consequences *do* often follow. If "the battle for full equality" is defined as necessarily including straight male approbation of gay male public displays of affection, I suspect it's a battle that will never be won. Inescapably, the sight of two men kissing conjures up related images and emotions—including the sheer terror (disguised as disgust) of picturing one man putting his penis into another man's asshole. The "filth" of excrement is automatically evoked but perhaps still worse psychologically is the image of a man being penetrated, dominated, *used* ("the way women are").

The affront is to the traditional male's insistence that the very essence of manliness resides in testosterone-fueled aggression. Anal sex is in fact characteristically the interaction of *two* active partners, not one aggressor and one passive recipient of aggression. No anal sex worth a candle involves a limp, passive, nearly comatose "victim"; *both* participants write the script, both actively orchestrate the scene, both gyrate their bodies with interactive abandon. Which fact, if acknowledged, would, as it were, make the traditional-minded heterosexual male's blood run cold (or, perhaps put more appropriately, scare the shit out of him).

If we retreat from expecting straight male approbation for gay male anal sex to the less fraught terrain of male-to-male tenderness and affection, we can take some comfort in history. As I've recounted in my memoir *The Rest of It,* in the early seventies I dug up a variety of documents in historical archives that recorded a level of heterosexual male-male intimacy largely unknown today. I'll limit myself here to two of the examples I describe in that book. The first is the astonishing forty-volume manuscript diary kept by a minor writer named F. S. Ryman and housed in the Massachusetts Historical Society. The material from the diary entries Ryman made in the 1880s, when he was living in upstate New York, is particularly germane.

Ryman's close friend, a hotel clerk named Rob Luke, came to stay with him one night, and Ryman described their interaction in his diary. "I confess," he wrote,

I like the oriental custom of men embracing & kissing each other if they are indeed dear friends. When we went to bed Rob put his arms around me & lay his head down by my right shoulder in the most loving way & then I put my arms around his neck & thus clasped in each other's arms we talked for a long time till we were ready to go to sleep & then we separated as I cannot sleep good with anyone near me. This a.m. Rob got up to go at 5 o'clock & as he was starting he came to the bed & threw his arms around my neck & we kissed each other good bye though I expect to see him again to-day. Now in all this I am certain there was no sexual sentiment on the part of either of us. We both have our mistresses whom we see with reasonable regularity & I am certain that the thought of the least demonstration of unmanly & abnormal passion would have been as revolting to him as it is & ever has been to me.

When I first discovered Ryman's diary, I published excerpts from it in a column I was then writing for the now-defunct gay paper the *New York Native*. In my commentary I suggested that most readers today would likely equate the passionate embraces of Ryman and Rob with erotic arousal. But that equation, I suggested, was in all likelihood unwarranted. In my view, I wrote, "their physical (as contrasted with genital) contact can probably best be explained as the function of a different set of conventions from ours about what are or aren't appropriate, permissible expressions of affection between two close male friends." I suggested further that the Ryman-Rob relationship raised some pertinent questions about just how "prudish" the Victorians in fact were—and just how "liberated" we are.

Today I'd amend that comment to add that in my experience gay male friends are *more* likely to embrace and kiss than they were in the early seventies, and straight male friends *less* likely even to *talk* intimately with each other. Quoting various studies, a recent article in the *New York Times* reported that "consciously or otherwise, many men believe that talking about personal matters with other men is not manly. The result is often less intimate, more casual friendships between men, making the connections more tenuous and harder to sustain." If intimate talk is increasingly tabooed among straight men, intimate *touching* is clearly beyond the pale.[4]

Jumping back to the *early* nineteenth century, I came upon several letters (now housed in the South Caroliniana Library) between two aristocratic young men that draws the contrast between then and now even more starkly. The 1826 exchange was between Jeff Withers and James ("Jim") Hammond—later one of the antebellum South's "great men" (and a prominent defender of black slavery). In a letter dated May 15, 1826, Jeff playfully wrote Jim that he felt "some inclination to learn whether you yet sleep in your Shirt-tail, and whether you yet have the extravagant delight of poking and punching a writhing Bedfellow with your long fleshen pole—the exquisite touches of which I have often had the honor of feeling." In a second letter, Jeff was still more spectacularly specific: "I fancy, Jim, that your *elongated protuberance*—your fleshen pole—has captured complete mastery over you—and I really believe, that you are charging over the pine barrens of your locality, braying, like an ass, at every she-male you can discover."

Both men, I should add, married and had children, and Hammond's sexual history was extravagant enough to include the attempted seduction of the teenage daughters of Wade Hampton, another of the South's "great men" (a deed that, when exposed, led Hampton to block Hammond's candidacy for the

U.S. Senate). In printing the letters in the *New York Native,* I raised the unanswerable question of whether we should regard Jeff's two letters as describing behavior viewed at the time as "anomalous or representative." Was it confined to the special relationship between Jeff and Jim, or did the letters represent a wider pattern of male-male intimacy "till now unsuspected and undocumented, yet in some sense 'typical' of their time, region, race, and class?" The answer, alas, was—and is: "We don't know. There's no comparable evidence in the correspondence of the period, or perhaps it hasn't yet surfaced." Which is precisely why the history of sexual behavior has since then become a necessary and popular field of study (though it has as yet yielded no answer to my question as posed).

If "the battle for full equality" must trim its expectations to exclude any hope of the heterosexual male sanctioning male-to-male intimacy (sexual or affectionate), there are other grounds entirely for wondering whether "full equality" is intrinsically an appropriate or feasible goal. Michelangelo Signorile, for one, argues that "what we truly need" is "a full civil rights bill ... that encompasses employment, housing, public accommodations, education, and all banking and lending, without a religious exemption any broader than the one in the Civil Rights Act of 1964. We must not settle for anything less."

I wonder. If we succeed in getting such legislation passed, what precisely will we have accomplished? Less discrimination on the public level? Yes, unquestionably, and well worth having. More freedom to be ourselves? Well, that's more problematic. It all depends on who "we" think we *are.* Our national organizations—preeminently the Human Rights Campaign, Lambda Legal Defense, GLAAD (Gay and Lesbian Alliance Against

Defamation), and the National Gay and Lesbian Task Force—seem to know, or act as if they do. The answer they tend to give, as deduced from their political activities, is that "we" are white, middle- and upper-class, straight-acting, upstanding patriots, devoted believers in the American way.

"We" (the Human Rights Campaign et al.) campaigned vigorously for the right to serve openly and without question in the armed forces. Once Congress decided it would allow us to join, how many of us in the appropriate age bracket presented ourselves for induction? Not many is my guess. Why not? Because joining the army isn't the high priority for many middle-class gay people that our national organizations apparently think it is. Reliable statistics, though, are hard to come by, probably because many low-income minority gays don't self-identify as queer, or prefer to remain closeted, and it's precisely on the low-income pool that our armed forces heavily rely for volunteers (since the military is low-income people's only prospect for a decent income and a possible career).

Between 1995 and 2014 the overall proportion of minorities in all branches of the service was 31 percent of the total—higher than the minority share of the population, and greater in 2014 than in 1995—with only 7 percent of the recruits having a bachelor's degree or higher. What share of that 31 percent was gay? There's no way to know. We don't even know what question we're seeking an answer to. Is it, Do you have sex with people of your own gender? Or, "Do you self-identify as 'gay,' even though you may sleep with people of both (or multiple) genders?" Yes, it gets complicated.

About all we can say with certainty is that the repeal of Clinton's egregious "Don't ask, don't tell" policy *did* open the way for lesbians and gays to volunteer for the armed forces. A campaign is afoot to end the exclusion of trans people—which, as of this writing, the Trump administration opposes—both on moral grounds and (as Signorile, for one, puts it) as a way of bringing the U.S. military "up to speed." Trans people should of course be allowed access to any and every institution they care to join. But how about an agenda *beyond* the right to volunteer for the potential killing fields? How about, for example, a campaign for *unilateral disarmament,* or perhaps an international ban on nuclear weapons? (Either would have been popular in GLF.) Impractical? Foolishly idealistic? That's what they told the abolitionists in the mid-nineteenth century. Humanitarian concerns are *always* dismissed as impractical, at least initially.

Humanitarian concerns, however, aren't high on the national gay movement's list of priorities; if they were, we'd hear a lot more from them than we do about the inequities that derive from race, class, and gender. The agenda of the Human Rights Campaign, the largest and wealthiest gay organization, is focused on gaining greater access to the institutions that dominate American life (for which one usually needs, as well, a certain level of education, along with specialized skills—which low-income gay people are unlikely to have). In pursuit of its agenda, HRC has utilized traditional political tools like electioneering, lobbying, and litigation, and its own organizational structure is a clue to the kind of issues it pursues: HRC has a hierarchical structure with an all-powerful executive board, and no local branches to hold it accountable to grassroots concerns (though in 2017 it did declare its intention to do more local organizing). Its strategy is what Signorile has aptly characterized as "incrementalist" ("winning a little bit at a time"), a political philosophy that accurately reflects the limitations of the "official" gay movement.

Signorile is—rightly, in my view—scornful of HRC's limited scope of engagement. He forcefully argues for an expanded set of demands, which he summarizes as "a broad and comprehensive civil rights bill"; and he wants it to be built on the kind of grass-roots-generated activity that carried the movement for marriage equality to a successful conclusion. He wants HRC to ask for "more" and he wants it to move at an accelerated speed. What he doesn't advocate is digging up the pavement and laying down a broader highway that a greater variety of vehicles would be able to traverse. Those vehicles are out there, but the dirt roads and the thick underbrush are hindering their visibility—and their forward movement. Signorile either doesn't know about them or regards them as too tangential to warrant discussion. He wants the large national organizations to pick up the beat, but not to add new songs to its repertoire. Despite his own radical past—his was the essential voice in the earlier campaign that "outed" public figures actively doing harm to gay people—Signorile seems content to keep riding along the same road, the one with a large signpost reading LIBERAL: Mainstream Friendly, Media Savvy.[5]

It's a narrative of progress that features a particular, and limited, set of issues: marriage equality, open service in the military, safe schools, adoption rights, antidiscrimination and hate crime legislation. The first two have been achieved (though not set to rest); the latter four remain controversial works in progress. A host of other matters that affect the lives of many LGBTQ people—among them, health care, senior centers, immigration, poverty, homelessness, diet, and education—are currently given short shrift. Even those issues still being partially addressed, like hate crime legislation, are of uncertain relevance (and even potential harm) to much of the queer population.

On the margins of the national gay movement, a number of radical individuals and grassroots organizations have for some time been actively protesting the national movement's "capture" of the gay agenda for marriage equality and military service at the expense of a large number of issues (like full-time, reliable jobs) of greater relevance to the majority of low-income gay people. Among these local groups—and low-income minorities of color, and trans people, are prominent in their leadership—are Southerners On New Ground (SONG), the Sylvia Rivera Law Project, the Audre Lorde Project, FIERCE, the LGBT Poverty Collective, Women of Color against Violence, and the recently closed Queers for Economic Justice (with which I myself was involved; QEJ's focus was on the rights of gay people living in shelters).

These local organizations are, as it were, the left wing of the gay rights movement, and they're playing a role comparable to the one that GLF played in the early seventies. Joseph DeFilippis, in his pioneering doctoral dissertation, has aptly called them the new "queer liberation movement." They're multi-issue organizations that stress coalition work and pay close attention—far more than the mainstream movement does—to the interlocking ("intersectional") sources of discrimination that derive not just from one's sexual orientation but from one's class, race, and gender as well. The primary focus of these local organizations is not on gaining access to established institutions but on radically changing—or possibly replacing—them.[6]

Most of these radical activists don't scorn, or wish to turn back the clock on, the recent increases in gay access to resources and recognition that have resulted from the mainstream gay movement's efforts. Yet, although they believe that it's essential to oppose legal discrimination of every kind, they aren't exactly cheerleaders for gay marriage or the right to serve openly in the military. (Mattilda Bernstein Sycamore, for one, has eloquently and contemptuously spoken of "the right to fight in unjust wars.")

In this regard, the sociologist Alan Sears has posed a fundamental question: Why is it that the gay movement has "made gains at a time when in fact most movements seeking change" have been "pushed backwards?" Sears cites in particular the ground lost in recent decades in the struggles for affirmative action, abortion rights, unionization, and immigration reform. He suggests that the gay movement has succeeded in gaining access to the institutions of marriage and military service because the powers-that-be welcome the addition of adherents to traditional institutions who help to *bolster* the current system of social control and domination that distributes large rewards to the relative few—and who *don't* raise the tough questions of who is left out of the prosperity mill and why. The gay movement's much-heralded advances of recent years have been, as Sears puts it, "the relatively easy stuff that fits with this system."[7]

The gay radicals of SONG and other local political formations are focusing on precisely those demands that are *not* compatible with capitalism, putting particular stress on issues relating to economic inequality. They insist on the importance of moving beyond the goal of mere "acceptance" into the established order, toward a substantive critique of what Lisa Duggan has called "homonormativity"—namely, the gay white middle-class focus on consumption and domesticity. The liberationists' goal is radical transformation, not liberal tinkering.

In her essay "After Gay Marriage" (2015), Kate Redburn cites various studies that demonstrate how queer poverty has become racialized. One survey of trans Latina women found "extremely low rates of employment and health insurance coverage and high rates of employment discrimination and poverty." Another study concluded that African American gay male couples are six times more likely to be poor than their white counterparts. Redburn also sounds a timely warning against the smugness of "Victory!" types like Andrew Sullivan. Homophobia, she makes clear, is alive and well, and is busily carving out all kinds of ingenious new strategies for holding "sick" gays at bay. A 2015 Harris poll revealed startling evidence of well-entrenched prejudice: a third of the respondents said they'd feel uncomfortable seeing a same-sex couple holding hands—roughly the same number that would be unhappy to learn that their doctor was gay. Running parallel to mounting bigotry is a *lessening* of activism in the gay community: only 4 percent of LGBTQ people donate to gay causes.[8]

The radical local gay groups at work sharply criticize the minimal attention the national gay organizations have been paying to a variety of problems that afflict low-income gay groups (as well as the general population, of course), in particular, prison reform and hate crime legislation. Dean Spade, the founder of the Sylvia Rivera Law Project and a professor at the Seattle University School of Law, has written forcefully about the issue of prison reform. "Given the severe anti-black racism of the criminal punishment system, what does it mean," Spade asks, "to call on that system for justice and accountability?" Opposition to the justice system, he argues, should include strenuous resistance to prison expansion. Currently there are some 2.3 million people in our jails; we lock up more citizens than any other country—with 5 percent of the world's population, we account for 25 percent of its prisoners.[9]

Blacks and Latinos, moreover, are wildly overrepresented in our prisons. Though together they make up 31 percent of the U.S. population, they're 59 percent of the prison population.

Two major new studies agree that harsh drug laws, racism, and a crackdown on nonviolent offenders, though significant factors in creating this disparity, have to some extent been overemphasized. Racial bias is unquestionably the key element in swelling our prison population, but too little attention has been paid, the new studies argue, to the role overzealous black leaders have played in an effort to reduce the inner-city scourges of crime and violence, and to the overly strict guidelines imposed on prosecutors in pushing tough-on-crime legislation. The only good news in this bleak picture is that a shift away from incarceration has begun, the imprisonment rate having dropped by 8 percent between 2010 and 2015.[10]

Still, the story remains bleak, and the mainstream gay organizations have played almost no role in the resistance to hiring more cops, building more jails, criminalizing more behaviors, and lengthening more sentences—though many gay citizens are suffering from the consequences. Nor have they, as Dean Spade persuasively argues, done much of anything to help disrupt "the cultural myths" that continue to describe our law enforcement system as a "justice system" and our police as devoted to "'protecting and serving' everyone." Spade may go too far—or perhaps the limits of my own radicalism are showing—when he insists that it's a "racist lie" "that *any* justice [the emphasis is mine] can emerge from prosecution and imprisonment."

Spade is surely right when he goes on to question the extent to which so-called hate crime legislation actually protects gay people from violence—though it most assuredly does further engorge our prisons. The 2010 Hate Crimes Prevention Act (widely known as the Matthew Sheppard Act) extended the definition of federal hate crime laws to include crimes targeting a victim for his or her "actual or perceived" gender, sexual orientation, gender identity, or disability. By the end of that same year most of the states had passed some form of hate crime legislation. To date, there's little evidence that these laws—which have unquestionably incarcerated more people and led to the building of more jails—have successfully reduced (as Spade puts it) "rape, child sexual abuse, poverty, police violence, racism, ableism, and the other things that are killing us."[11]

What alternative policies *might* make us safer? Here Spade grows vaguer—necessarily perhaps, since the root causes of violence, such as homophobia, aren't susceptible of easy cures. (And perpetrators of child sexual abuse, for example, are more often than not family members.) Spade urges a shift of attention from jailing "sex offenders" to making greater efforts to work against the social violence of everyday life among the most vulnerable among us—children, say, or trans people—and to providing direct support, for example, to homeless queer people and those subject to deportation. As our prison system stands, it doesn't help prisoners, many of whom are incarcerated for minor offenses (like being caught with a little pot), and it apparently doesn't make the rest of us any safer. What might? Improving the wretched conditions under which so many people, gay and straight, live—in overcrowded shelters (or on the street), eating cheap unhealthy food, never being able to afford a doctor's visit or to sustain viable networks of friendship and support.

One LGBTQ radical activist has argued that "putting our energy toward promoting harsher sentencing takes it away from the more difficult and more important work of changing our culture so that no one wants to kill another person because of their perceived membership in a marginalized identity group."[12] We could use a few more specifics, of course, about how to "change our culture," and can perhaps be excused for wondering in what distant millennium that change is likely to occur. In the interim, I think it's fair to question whether the evidence that hate crime laws don't reduce hate crimes is airtight. At the least, don't such laws publicly announce that homophobia, transphobia, and other forms of hatred are now declared outside the realm of acceptable, moral behavior—and isn't that announcement worth having?

Hate crimes law can't overnight erase, or in the short run even diminish, violent bigotry, but the literature on prejudice does suggest that over the long haul laws *can* influence behavior and that legally enforced, repetitive changes in behavior, even minimal ones, do ultimately accumulate to the point that—with the exception of the most committed haters among us—*our belief systems* also change. While working toward and awaiting (the possibly illusory) time when we will live in a transformed culture, is it sufficient to say, as radical activist Yasmin Nair does, that jailing people for bigoted behavior will "just end up policing thought and filling the coffers of the prison industrial complex"? She may be right, but I don't believe that the sketchy evidence we have to date about the effectiveness (or lack thereof) of hate crime laws warrants a definitive closing of the books on the subject.[13]

Gay chauvinism—and I've sometimes indulged in it—has as its centerpiece the notion that our outsider status has provided us with a set of values and perspectives at odds with (as the chauvinists see it) the hypocrisy and shortcomings of mainstream American life, and in particular American male culture. That assumption, in my opinion, needs far more scrutiny than it usually gets. There's considerable evidence for claiming that—speaking broadly and acknowledging the many variations in individual experience—a distinctive set of values *has* emerged in the gay world. The claim has mostly been cast in a positive light. The outsider perspective, it's said, has given LGBTQ people in general unique and valuable insights into the human condition not available to the bourgeois mainstream and, further, gay subcultural values could—if given the chance—greatly enrich conventional norms.

In regard to gay male life specifically, a number of academic studies have concluded that we're more emotionally expressive and sexually innovative than heterosexual men, more empathic, and more altruistic (we do volunteer work far more often than our straight male counterparts), and we're more likely to cross racial and gender borders when forming close bonds of friendship. When part of a couple, we—and this is even more true of lesbian partnerships—avoid stereotypic gender roles and instead emphasize mutuality and shared responsibilities. Gay couples have "more relationship satisfaction" than straight couples, and when we do argue, we're better at seeing our partner's point of view and at using humor to deflate belligerence. As the *New York Times* put it in summarizing a number of the recent studies, same-sex couples are "far more egalitarian" than our heterosexual counterparts and in this regard "have a great deal to teach everyone else."[14]

The case for gay chauvinism usually stops there, and if the story already sounds too good to be true, it probably is. A couple, after all, is made up of two individuals (leaving aside for the moment polygamous, polyandrous, and polyamorous relationships), and as many studies have concluded, the single gay person is often chronically stressed and troubled, his or her pain deep enough to make us skeptical that it could simply disappear after entering into a relationship. Yet if gay coupledom isn't necessarily a bower of bliss, being single *is* more likely to involve (especially for gay men) substance abuse and dangerous sexual encounters—and the attendant mood disorders and anxiety that often accompany them. In comparison to heterosexuals, all the studies on suicide have drawn the same conclusion: LGBTQ individuals have markedly higher rates than heterosexuals.[15]

The empirical data provide no evidence for any claim that these health disparities are linked to some intrinsic genetic predisposition. Instead, the explanation for higher rates of certain physical and emotional disorders among gay people is social; they're the by-products of prejudice, discrimination, victimization, and rejection, as well as the coping mechanisms developed to contain them—including concealment, distrust, and internalized homophobia. Some evidence also suggests that such "stressors" are directly linked to elevated levels of cardiovascular disease, asthma, and diabetes in the gay community. Comparable stressors are higher than average among all racial and sexual minorities (60 percent of African Americans also experience some form of social rejection—and in consequence a heightened level of chronic anxiety).

The rebuttal that "life is hard for everybody"—that existential angst is the very definition of consciousness—can sometimes lead to the false equivalency that dismisses "minority stressors" as simply part of the price we pay for being alive. The point shouldn't have to be made, but the price for some is higher than for others, the pain out of all proportion to the pleasure. Curiously, the denial of suffering is pronounced within the gay community itself. The difficulties of a gay lifestyle have generally been glossed over as inconvenient when waving the banner of Gay Pride (that glib, ubiquitous phrase that regularly alternates with the equally fatuous "Gay Is Good"). That sort of self-aggrandizing sloganeering is a disservice on several levels: since life is hard for damned-near everybody, it suggests that we're somehow immune—rather than uncommonly susceptible—to the everyday hazards of being alive. It also keeps us from acknowledging to ourselves the particular pitfalls of being gay—an essential first step in learning how to cope with them. Without doubt, there's much to affirm and even celebrate about gay life, as I've already itemized (the greater mutuality and satisfaction that characterize our coupled relationships, the greater empathy and altruism that gay men exhibit compared to heterosexual men, etc.). However, to *exclusively* stress its positive aspects—"the politics of affirmation"—amounts to the kind of denial intrinsically bound up with the bland assertion, so commonplace these days, that we're just as "normal" as everybody else—and to be normal in the American bowl-of-cherries version of reality means to be problem-free (or to pretend to be). The pretense that our lives are untroubled is a double disservice to *ourselves:* if nothing's wrong, we have no incentive to better understand the source of our pain or to seek constructive ways for alleviating it—nor to understand and hold accountable "the *structures* of society" (as Toby Manning has put it) responsible for the "minority stress" we sometimes suffer from.[16] In a troubling recent essay, "The Epidemic of Gay Loneliness," Michael Hobbes has cast further light on the extent of that stress. In doing so, however, he's focused exclusively on the experience of privileged white men, ignoring possible points of comparison with the lives of lesbians and people of color. Still, what Hobbes tells us about that subset of privileged white men—those who, from at least a material point of view, should be among our most contented folks—illuminates some unsettling aspects of gay male life we typically ignore.[17]

Hobbes cites John Pachankis, a stress researcher at Yale, who believes that in regard to gay people, the greatest damage gets done "in the five or so years between realizing your sexuality and starting to tell other people." The felt need to be constantly on guard, the fear of slipping up and revealing too much, takes a long-term toll, both psychologically and physically. And that toll doesn't simply disappear after we've grown into adulthood and "accepted" or revealed our sexuality (for some, guilt, shame, and regret remain omnipresent). If during adolescence we spend a good deal of psychic energy on concealing who we are from other people, including our families, our capacity for trust and intimacy alike can become permanently compromised.

Which would mean, among other things, that we might not be as good at friendship as we often claim. "We don't need traditional families," goes the common mantra; "we have our friendship networks," and they're *better* than traditional families because they aren't weighed down by the remnants from childhood of sibling rivalry or the grievances relating to parental control. Maybe so. In some cases, certainly. But the overall quality of gay male friendship, as Hobbes reports, isn't particularly attractive. Over and over he hears the story of the young gay man arriving in, say, New York City who feels he'll "finally be accepted" for who he is and who discovers that although he isn't rejected for being gay, he *is* rejected for his weight, his income, or his race. One of Hobbes's young informants tells him that "the bullied kids of our youth grew up and became bullies themselves." Another simply decides that "gay men in particular are just not very nice to each other." Hobbes believes that "'in-group discrimination' does more harm to your psyche than getting rejected by members of the majority," because it feels as if you've lost "your only way of making friends and finding love. Being pushed away from your own people hurts more because you need them more."

The result, Hobbes claims, is that unlike other minority groups whose members find that "living in a community with people like them is linked to lower rates of anxiety and depression," it's the opposite for gay men. Hobbes cites "several studies"—though he fails to name them—that found "living in gay neighborhoods predicts higher rates of risky sex and meth use and less time spent on other community activities like volunteering or playing sports." Perhaps that conclusion might not sound to me as shaky as it does if Hobbes had cited the comparative experience of other minorities. Do young black men find less rejection from their peers in Harlem, have lower rates of "risky sex and meth use," and spend *more* time doing community volunteering? On all counts, I very much doubt it.

What I don't doubt is the pervasive stigma in gay male enclaves against "feminine guys." Here Hobbes *does* cite some studies, and they do uniformly back up his conclusion that "feminine" gay men turn out to be more at risk for suicide, loneliness, and mental illness. Yet according to Hobbes, "masculine" (we could do with some definitions here) gay men in fact indulge in "risky" sex and use drugs *more* than "effeminate" gay men do—and have higher levels of anxiety. Which leads us to conclude—what? That their muscular desirability and the admiration it engenders keep them this side of suicidal affect? Something in Hobbes's analysis seems awry.

He does seem on target when blaming social media—and the concomitant disappearance of traditional gay spaces like bars and bathhouses—for much of the anxiety he finds in the gay male community. He thinks the "hookup apps" like Grindr, where the majority of gay men now meet each other, are particularly potent stressors—they're "almost perfectly designed to underline our negative beliefs about ourselves ... [they're] an efficient way to feel ugly"—yet Hobbes doesn't say precisely how or why. He seems to be suggesting that everyone is looking for the same thing: a partner who's "tall, young, white, muscular, and masculine," and "the vast majority of us ... barely meet one of those criteria, much less all five." So? People *do* meet online, and some of them find long-term partners there. How can that be if the odds are truly so small? The effect of hookup apps, and social media in general, needs more thorough-going discussion.

The formative five-year period between realizing your sexuality and starting to tell other people about it seems the true seeding ground for adult gay male loneliness and depression. Emily Greytak (director of research for the Gay, Lesbian, Straight Education Network, or GLSEN) and her associates have revealed that from 2005 to 2015 "the percentage of teenagers who said they were bullied for their sexual orientation didn't fall at all." The schools remain dangerous places for young people trying to come to terms with their sexuality. Apparently only some 30 percent of school districts in the country have anti-bullying policies that specifically mention LGBTQ kids, and thousands of districts bar teachers from speaking positively about homosexuality. Teenagers who feel rejected are more likely to self-medicate with increasingly dangerous drugs, to have unprotected sex when high, and then, to avoid despondency when coming down, turn to still more drugs and still greater risks. As the repetitive process deepens, they grow increasingly out of touch with their feelings—if they stay alive—and emotional detachment becomes a prominent feature of their personalities.[18]

For a more *comprehensive* understanding of the causal factors behind the high incidence of gay loneliness and depression, we need—so it seems to me—to go beyond Michael Hobbes's "formative five-year period" and seek more foundational roots in contemporary theories of child development. Currently, the literature on the emotional problems in the gay population largely ignores the insights of "attachment theory," associated with John Bowlby, Mary Ainsworth, and Donald Winnicott—though their work is held in high regard in psychoanalytic circles. As a nonspecialist, I can at best only begin to suggest the potential relevance of attachment theory for a better understanding of the widespread incidence of loneliness, gay or otherwise.

Attachment theory places primary emphasis on the critical importance for young children of strong physical and emotional bonds with their primary caretakers. Should the caregiver not respond to the youngster's spontaneous actions and expressions of feeling in a welcoming, reassuring way, the development of the child's confident sense of self is jeopardized.

Similarly, if negative interactions occur—the primary caretaker's disappearance, say, or a father's expressed disgust with his son's effeminacy—the impact can produce adverse and long-term repercussions in a child's emotional life. Disrupted or failed attachments do not in themselves produce either straight or gay children, but they do painfully augment the extent of adult suffering.

We need to remain wary of linking certain aspects of a child's upbringing with specific sexual orientation outcomes. The discredited theories of Irving Bieber and Charles Socarides, which blamed the "pathology" of homosexuality on certain "unhealthy" family configurations, produced in gay people a horrendous amount of self-distrust—and ever since the subject of "causality" has been tabooed in gay circles. But this may be a case of throwing the baby out with the bath. The terrain *is* treacherous, but if Hobbes is correct and gay men experience far more loneliness and depression than do straight men, we need to find out why. And the search for an explanation may require us to retrieve the subject of child development from the discard pile. We cannot ameliorate what we do not understand.

Hobbes, for one, doubts that "we'll ever see the mental health gap between straight people and gay people close, at least not fully." We'll always be in a small minority, he argues, isolated in our families, our schools, and our towns. He tries hard to put a positive gloss on it: "Our distance from the mainstream may be the source of some of what ails us, but it is also the source of our wit, our resilience, our empathy, our superior talents." Is this a trade-off we should simply resign ourselves to? If the "source" of our isolation and depression lies in society's lethal mistreatment of us—and it mostly does—why don't we, as they did in GLF, wake up politically, mobilize our collective strength, and actively assail the engulfing walls of prejudice that enclose us— and that do show signs of weakening and decay? Controversial though the findings are regarding LGBTQ "mental health," one conclusion *is* obvious: Gay Is Not Yet Good Enough. The suffering goes on, and at high levels—and Gay Pride should be seen as an aspiration, not a settled accomplishment.

When GLF talked about sexual liberation, the agenda often included two interlocking items rarely mentioned these days: freeing up same-sex attraction in confirmed heterosexuals and releasing heterosexual desire in those who considered themselves exclusively gay. They talked, in other words, about the currently marginal topic of bisexuality. Not everyone joined the choir back then, but a number of voices did tout bisexuality (along with androgyny) as the gold standard for membership in the cultural vanguard. In a 1974 article in the newspaper the *Gay Alternative*, Phil Mullen, speaking for many, wrote: "We gay people have often been heard to argue that the lives of straights would be richer if they could only respond sexually and emotionally to others of their own gender. Our gay lives, by the same token, would be richer if we could open up to ... heterosexual love.... Now that we're finally learning that gay is good, we'll have to start learning that gay isn't good enough."[19]

Today, a view like Mullen's runs directly counter to the common attitude among older adults that one is *either* gay or straight, that biology has predetermined a binary division, that self-proclaimed bisexuals are people *in transition* to firm membership in one category or another—that in the meantime they're being either cowardly or stubbornly contrary. Many in the younger generation feel, rather unexpectedly, otherwise.

In an illuminating 2015 article in the *New York Times*, Charles Blow summarized the sizable and growing generation gap on the question of erotic fluidity. Using the familiar Kinsey scale of 0 to 6 (0 being exclusively heterosexual, and 6 exclusively homosexual), Blow cites a British survey that found a full 43 percent of eighteen-to-twenty-four-year-olds place themselves between 1 and 5—that is, bisexual—while 52 percent locate themselves at one end of the spectrum or the other (46 percent describing themselves as entirely straight and 6 percent entirely gay). A comparable American survey has revealed that 29 percent of those within the age range eighteen to twenty-nine expressed some degree of bisexual attraction—as compared with the forty-five-to-sixty-four age group in which a mere 8 percent felt that way. Younger people are clearly describing their sexuality in far more fluid terms than their elders. When Miley Cyrus calls herself "pansexual," she's speaking for a growing number of her contemporaries—though they may chose different descriptive words, such as *omnisexual, polyamorous, polyromantic*—or *asexual*. The times they *are* a-changin'.[20]

As to how much they're changing, considerable disagreement reigns among the "experts." Few of them seem familiar with historical, anthropological, or primate studies, yet all three areas of research throw considerable light on the issue. In regard to animal studies, the zoologist R. H. Dennison long ago declared categorically that "frequent homosexual activity has been described for all species of mammals of which careful observations have been made [and] it has little relation to hormonal or structural abnormality."[21]

Despite Dennison, the scientific community has continued to express its discomfort with the subject of sex by waving it away as simply the motor force behind an evolutionary urge to reproduce. When faced with evidence of same-gender sexuality in the animal kingdom, scientists tend to dismiss it as "pseudocopulation" done under "abnormal conditions." This sort of avoidance can no longer pass muster—thanks to the publication in 1999 of Bruce Bagemihl's *Biological Exuberance: Animal Homosexuality and Natural Diversity*, followed by Joan Roughgarden's equally brilliant *Evolution's Rainbow: Diversity, Gender, and Sexuality in Nature and People*. As a result, the scientific community has now become less vocal about referring to same-gender sexuality in the animal kingdom as "unfortunate" or "inappropriate"—yet the bias remains very much in evidence.[22]

One obvious caution is in order. As I wrote back in 1974, "Extrapolations from animal behavior to human behavior tend to be simplistic and misleading. We can tell plainly enough when two stumptail male monkeys are pleasuring each other (in eight observable positions, no less)," but we can't be sure whether and how the artificial environment of the laboratory is affecting the behavior; whether and how the feelings of scientists observing those prodigious instances of fellatio and sodomy are affecting their "objective" reporting of them; and "whether, indeed, the behavior of the stumptail monkey has much of *anything* to do with that, say, of macaque baboons, let alone with that of the inhabitants of New York City."[23]

Anthropological findings, which deal directly with human behavior, are less subject to question. For several decades now, they've clustered firmly around the conclusion that human sexual behavior primarily derives from culturally learned norms, not instinctual imperatives. Evidence available as far back as the early seventies demonstrated (as I then wrote) that "we're capable of seeking pleasure and relatedness wherever our socially conditioned psyches cue us to look for them.... Even a cursory glance at other cultures confirms the dependency of our own psychosexual patterns on parochial and largely tacit social dictates." More than fifty years ago Clellan Ford and Frank Beach, in their epochal book *Patterns of Sexual Behavior,* revealed that forty-nine of the seventy-six societies they surveyed (64 percent) viewed male homosexuality as a normal sexual adaptation; some 17 percent of the societies also sanctioned female homosexuality—though in anthropology, as in the rest of the social sciences, female behavior has been less studied.[24]

The forty-nine societies that sanctioned male homosexuality varied widely in the particular acts they approved, in the degree those acts were institutionalized, and the extent to which they were simply tolerated or actually prescribed. The variations between cultures are enormous. In the New Guinea highlands, the Kukukuku people insist upon adolescent boys regularly ingesting adult male semen as *the* essential ingredient for virile growth. Alternatively, the Keraki of New Guinea prescribe regularized anal penetration by the adult male of the young boy. And in the Melanesian culture, sexual partnerships between adolescent males (even brothers) is commonplace.

In all these instances—and they could be multiplied many times over—the participants are *not* engaging exclusively in same-sex acts. Upon growing up, the young males are expected to form opposite-gender attachments, to produce families of their own, and as adults, to provide their semen to the "needy" young. In these cultures exclusive, lifetime male homosexuality is apparently unknown; the more accurate description of their pattern might be "serial bisexuality." Historically, moreover, evidence of widespread bisexual behavior among men (women, again, have been studied less) is abundant—so much so that we would have to rank it, statistically, as among the few constants in male gender behavior, on a par with waging war or using intoxicants.

This should come as no surprise, since nothing in our biology inhibits our taking physical pleasure and emotional comfort from people of either gender. Though we have records for only about 1 percent of human history (until 10,000 years ago we lived in nonliterate hunting-and-gathering societies), evidence of bisexual behavior can be found in the Upanishads and the Old Testament—and certain Egyptian gods were notorious for their varied sexual choices. In the fourth century B.C. an elite band of male lovers died to a man in battling Philip of Macedon at Chaeronea. We also know that Sappho's poems were celebrated throughout the Greek world, and statues erected in her honor. Thanks to the advent of Christianity, homophobia supplanted bisexuality; at the Council of Constantinople (A.D. 390), the Christian emperor Theodosius saw to it that homosexuality was declared a capital crime.[25]

The emperor's views remain familiar. My own impression is that homophobia (at least in the West) has assuredly lessened—though hardly disappeared. My further hunch is that there's even less acceptance of bisexuality than homosexuality. Binary thinking still holds strong sway with the general population, and the exclusive homosexual is more understandable to the average person than is an individual who wanders the Kinsey scale with apparent—and alarming—abandon. In the Cartesian West, as I wrote some forty years ago, we've long been taught to think in either-or categories, to believe that one is male *or* female, boss *or* worker, teacher *or* student, child *or* adult, gay *or* straight. To suggest, as practicing bisexuals do, that each of us may contain within ourselves all of those supposed opposites we've been taught to divide humanity into is to suggest that we might not know ourselves as well as we like to pretend—and to suggest, too, that the roles by which most of us define ourselves represent transient, even outmoded social values, limitations imposed on us by the culture in which our worldview has evolved.

These days, especially within queer theory's hallowed halls, sexual "fluidity" has become something of a talisman for personal authenticity. Of course it's long been taken as a truism—probably an exaggerated one—that the gay bathhouses, rent-a-boy services, and online Grindr-like sites are haunted by married men determined to get their quota of (anonymous) gay sex. Yet I'd suggest that at least these "bisexual" men are consciously in touch with their need for sex with other men, whereas in earlier decades they might have hidden the information even from themselves.

A classic example of the bad old days is the material that emerged in William Masters and Virginia Johnson's 1979 book, *Homosexuality in Perspective.* It contains data on *un*conscious bisexuality that proved (though Master and Johnson were them-selves blind to it) spectacularly subversive—and to some, there-fore, deeply alarming. Over a twenty-year period, Masters and Johnson had gathered material about the fantasy lives of the four groups of informants they studied—homosexual men and women, heterosexual men and women—and they found a sur-prisingly high incidence of "cross-preference" fantasies. Hetero-sexual interaction was the third-highest fantasy among gay men and lesbians, and gay sex was only slightly lower than that for straight men and women.[26]

What made the findings especially remarkable was the fact that over the course of multiple interviews, the heterosexual subjects had self-described as Kinsey zeros—that is, exclusively straight—and had consistently expressed the view that same-gender sex was "revolting" and "unthinkable." Yet despite their carefully cen-sored sexual fantasies and their vitriolic homophobia, the same-sex desires of these superstraight subjects revealed, as Masters and Johnson put it, "a significant curiosity, a sense of sexual antici-pation, or even fears for effectiveness of sexual performance." M & J scrupulously avoided the scandalous implications of their own findings, sternly warning—their own homophobia show-ing—against the assumption that the "cross-preference" fantasies they'd uncovered indicated "latent or unrealized" homosexual attractions.

Really? Then what *did* those fantasies represent? M & J pro-vided no alternative interpretation and (as I wrote when review-ing their book) "it strains neither the evidence nor the imagina-tion to see in the high incidence of cross-preference fantasies confirmation of Freud's hoary suggestion that all human beings are potentially receptive to bisexual stimulation, that even when we have grown up in a homophobic culture and have long since declared ourselves gay or straight, the wish to be both retains a strong subterranean hold."[27]

Some forty years later, open experimentation has become far more widespread, with celebrities tripping over each other in grabbing the mike to broadcast their availability for a pachyderm three-way (while balancing on the trampoline). These days, an old-fashioned tumble in the hay with *a* member of the same sex is about as newsworthy as crossing the Atlantic in an airplane. But hold on. The shift in attitudes hasn't been across the board, and our sexological experts are themselves still divided as to where the erotic boundaries of the American psyche are currently located. What's considered acceptable in the larger cities isn't in traditional rural areas; sex involving teenagers is still widely regarded as "child molestation"; and men are not diving into the stream of fluidity with the same speed or zest as women.

One study reports that between 1973 and 1990 the percentage of adults who believed "sexual relations between two adults of the same sex was not wrong at all" only rose from 11 to 13 percent, but then from 1991 to 2014 the figures jumped way up: 49 percent of all adults and 63 percent of Millennials expressed "tolerance of these relations." "Tolerance"? Who chose the word—those doing the study or those studied? We aren't told. To me, at any rate, the word connotes a touch of residual contempt—and should forewarn us against assuming a conscious willingness to experiment with a gay partner.[28]

Matters become more complicated still regarding the much-debated phenomenon of bisexuality. A 2013 Pew Research Center study reported that 33 percent of its respondents claimed "a lot of social acceptance" for bisexual women, but only 9 percent for bisexual men. Back in 2005, moreover, a team of psychologists from two universities produced a study that cast doubt on whether bisexuality even *existed* among men. Basing their research on genital arousal patterns (while watching pornographic movies), they concluded that three-quarters of the men in the study who'd declared themselves bisexual in fact had the same arousal patterns as gay men—thus throwing doubt on whether bisexuality was a distinct or stable identity.[29]

Other researchers promptly denounced the study. Six years later, a team at Northwestern University drew the exact opposite conclusion: male bisexuality, they announced, is real. But the skeptics were unmoved. The gay conservative Andrew Sullivan, for one, continued to insist that "male sexuality is much cruder, simpler and more binary than female" and that men who claimed a bisexual orientation were simply using "a classic bridging mechanism to ease the transition" to their true identity—which was gay. Celebs Alan Cumming and Cynthia Nixon have since then joined the fray; though both are currently involved in long-term same-sex relationships, both insist that they remain attracted to opposite-gender people as well.

Meantime, still more studies are emerging that support the reality of bisexuality, some even claiming that bisexuals outnumber exclusive hets and homos (Kinsey o's and 6's). As if matters weren't complicated enough, one researcher has insisted on a definition that incorporates more than clitoral or penal excitation, claiming that measuring genital arousal alone "is too crude to capture the richness—the erotic sensations, affection, admiration—that constitutes sexual attraction." What?! Who knew that affection and admiration were prominent, even necessary, components of lust? Mystery and danger, yes—but *affection?*[30]

In this muck of controversy, yet another debate has arisen: the comparative sexual fluidity of men and women. The general assumption for some time has been that women "go back and forth" much more frequently than men do—including more lesbians than gay men. One 2015 University of Essex study went so far as to claim that "no woman is totally straight." Using eye-tracking devices and direct measures of physiological sexual response, Gerult Rieger, who led the study, concluded that although "the majority of women identified as straight, our research shows that, when it comes to what turns them on they are usually bisexual or gay, but never totally straight!" (*his* exclamation point).[31]

Not so fast, countered several other researchers. Lisa Diamond, a leading expert on the subject (and the author of the 2008 book *Sexual Fluidity*), found that many women experienced—some even against their conscious will—periodic shifts in gender attraction. But then Diamond gave a paper at the 2014 Society for Personality and Social Psychology Sexuality Preconference entitled "I Was Wrong! Men's Sexuality Is Pretty Darn Fluid Too." She has now come to believe, apparently, that a substantial number of women *and* men are sexually fluid—though heterosexual men much less so than heterosexual women: 24 percent of the straight men, but 50 percent of the straight women, reported having recently experienced some same-sex attraction. Lesbians and gay men registered comparable figures: 31 percent of the men and 42 percent of the women had masturbated to an opposite-sex fantasy recently.

The psychotherapist Joe Kort has added yet another wrinkle: fluidity, he claims, manifests differently for men and women. As a result of being "rigidly de-feminized" starting at an early age, boys learn to disassociate tenderness from sex. Where a bisexual woman might say, "It's not the gender, it's the person," a fluid man would be much more likely to say, "Hey, if my dick likes it, I'm going to go for it." Women, in other words, are more relational: they *combine*—while men separate—emotions and sex.

Which further means that men navigate casual sex more easily—and helps to explain why backroom orgy bars and bathhouses have long been features of gay male, but not lesbian, culture.[32]

"De-feminizing" may be the key concept—that is, unless one is wedded to a deterministic biological theory for male-female and gay-lesbian differences. Years ago I read somewhere—was it Donald Winnicott?—an explanation for male-female differences that has long stayed with me, and that I still find compelling. It goes something like this: in early childhood the mother and her female surrogates are the principal figures in bringing up *both* little boys and their sisters. But somewhere between ages five and eight, the men in the family take over. They figuratively yank the little boy away from the women, announcing (vocally or subliminally) that it's time to hang out with the *important* people—men. Through both their actions and their words, they let the little boy know that it's time to "give up all that girly stuff and learn to behave like a 'real' man." The effect on the boy can be deeply unsettling; having (in the best parenting scenario) worshipped his mother and relied on her for comfort and support, he's now being told that she and other women are of strictly secondary importance.

Little girls aren't subjected in a parallel way to having their early idols smashed, with the shards strewn throughout their adult lives; their mothers usually retain their unbroken stature as guides and models—which means that they're not psychologically subject to the boy's jolting, forced severance from his initially adored source of nurturance. He tries to cover over this profoundly wounding rupture using the new set of prescriptions being handed to him for "appropriate" male behavior. But the wound, no matter how deeply hidden under scar tissue, remains consequential. It's no wonder that during the World War II Blitz of London, men broke down under the strain far more often than women did.[33]

In her provocative book *Not Gay: Sex between Straight White Men,* Elizabeth Jane Ward reports on a new phenomenon that's recently emerged among the young: "heteroflexibility"—that is, "I'm straight, but shit happens." It's not clear how widespread the phenomenon is, but those who've joined its ranks apparently reject the label *bisexual*—since it implies a wavering identity— and heteroflexibles insist on their *un*wavering heterosexuality. To them, sexual orientation is biological in origin and their heterosexuality is *constitutional*—fixed. Various studies show that some college-age men, though rejecting the label "bisexual," are willing to describe themselves as "mostly" (rather than exclusively) heterosexual. What they mean, it seems, is that they see themselves as available for the unexpected "lark" of a homosexual encounter, justifying it as a superior capacity for openness and being game for expanded experience—but *not* as an intrinsic piece of their core identity. They know they're not gay, because (they tell themselves) they don't *love* other men; they don't confuse sex with romance, as truly gay men purportedly do.[34]

This doesn't mean that we're obligated to take these heteroflexibles at their word. Those theorists committed to a view of human sexuality centered on the concept of "polymorphous perversity" might well argue that young college men who subject themselves to the common fraternity hazing ritual of the "elephant walk"—during which naked young men form a chain by inserting a thumb into the anus of the man in front of him— are unconsciously acting out otherwise unacceptable homosexual urges while managing to escape the onus of adopting a gay identity.

Yet for heteroflexibles the imperative conviction that one is *not* gay overwhelms the behavioral evidence of the elephant walk. Even a specialist like Lisa Diamond (author of *Sexual Fluidity*) sees no contradiction between joining a fraternity ritual of "obvious" homoerotic overtones and seeing sexual orientation as hard-wired, a biological given. It helps to believe, as growing numbers of Americans (including Diamond) do, that sexual orientation, like race, is inborn. The proportion of those who believe in a biological explanation for sexual orientation has risen from a mere 13 percent in 1977 to 52 percent in 2010.

Yet the majority of academic specialists and intellectuals haven't joined that particular bandwagon. Any number of them, given the incomplete nature of our knowledge, are willing to pay at least pro forma lip service to the possibility that some unknown combination of genes and hormones interacts with unspecified environmental circumstances to create sexual desire. But that's a long way from saying that we know enough to elevate a possibility to a certainty; given the shifting, tumultuous inner whirlpool of individual desire, we may never know enough to be able to identify and concretely link causal elements to particular behaviors, sexual or otherwise.

What about the men in Jane Ward's *Not Gay?* An outside observer watching them "perform" the homoerotically charged elephant walk might be tempted to question their absolutist claim to heterosexuality. But the men themselves are in no doubt; for them it's a tough-guy ritual (like the way bikers kiss each other); they deny having any conscious fantasies about wanted to have "gay" sex, or the slightest identification with gay culture and politics. The same is true for the men who self-describe as heteroflexible; getting or giving a drunken blow job is to them simply seizing upon an unexpected opportunity to learn more about ways to pleasure the body. They delight in their self-image as a particular kind of straight men: antic, resilient, exploratory—happy-go-lucky daredevils, psychic spelunkers open to the excitement of behaving "incorrectly." According to this scenario, homosexual acts are not in themselves indictors to any degree of a homosexual orientation.

Which leads us—where? Jane Ward acutely formulates both the question and some possible, if somewhat opaque, answers. How do heterosexual men, she asks, "far from falling victim to an exceptional circumstance, learn to re-signify homosexual sex as an act of heteronormativity"? Her main interest (and mine) is how better to understand "what actually sets straight and queer lives apart." Part of her answer is connected to an insight that derives from a queer studies perspective: what defines homosexuality isn't same-gender sex, but rather "a refusal of gender and sexual normativity"—in other (Foucauldian) words, a particular (queer) way of being in the world.

Having persuasively formulated what's at stake, Ward goes on, in my reading of *Not Gay*, to expound what is to me an exaggerated presentation of the *normative* white male's way of life. She defines the key components of that life as a sense of racial superiority, political and economic entitlement (true of working-class whites too?), emotional invulnerability in tandem with a quickness to anger, misogyny, gendered violence, and homophobia. Underlying all that, presumably, is the ultimate, overwhelming need white men have to bond. Yet *is* that need, I'm left wondering, as strong as Ward claims? *Is* male bonding the primordial driving force—more than, say, reproductive sex or a simulated return to the womb? And why does male bonding necessitate actual homosexual contact?

These are the kind of questions I most loathe. They require a metaphysics whose necessity I've never understood, and an opaque use of language that I do my best to avoid. (My apologies to Jane Ward if I've misread or misused her often-stimulating words.) Plus I need to register yet one more doubt: to my mind it would have been sufficient for Ward to establish (as she convincingly does) that "grossness, anality, and the homoerotic" are unmistakable elements in normative white hetero-masculinity without going on to claim that they're among its "central ingredients." Her dissection of fraternity and military hazing rituals, pornography, biker clubs, and online personal ads is daring and effective. The doubt sets in only when she leaps, without sufficient explanation or (to my mind) justification, from ascribing activities that I consider marginal to the white male heterosexual world as a whole to the entirety of that world (as when she refers to "the sexism and boredom of heterosexuality").

All of our relationships, gay or straight, are tinged with sexism: we're not brought up on Mars. Also, I know plenty of heterosexuals who don't *seem* to find their lives boring—and at least as many homosexuals who *do* lament the sameness, the intolerable ennui, of their routinized relationships. We make a great mistake, it seems to me, when we narrowly disdain other people's choices or glorify our own as somehow superior; that sort of patronization comes alarmingly close to *hetero*phobia and, strangely, to a denial of our own suffering selves.

I hear that note of superiority sounded again when Ward describes "both heterosexual and mainstream gay culture [as] distasteful and often pitiable." In justifying so belittling a view, she resorts to descriptions of the oppositional queer counterculture in terms both glowing and suspiciously abstract: "Queerness directs its loving and lusting collective gaze at precisely the bodies and ways of life disavowed by straights as ugly and failed." I don't understand. *Which* straights are rejecting "precisely" *what* bodily aspects or elements of queer (as opposed to gay) lifestyles as "ugly" or "failed"? Nor do I understand Ward's declared "fetish for insubordinate bodies"—what presentations or actions are those bodies engaged in that earns them the affectionate label "insubordinate"? I yield nothing to Ward in my distaste for mainstream gay culture's turn to domesticity, family life, and upstanding citizenship, nor in my conviction that queerness holds the potential for the needed subversion of stereotypical gender and sexual behavior. But both the distaste and the conviction need more than blanket assertion; they need concrete evidence to back the claims, and crystal-clear arguments to sustain them.

One place to look for both is the current scientific debate about the workings of the brain. This is perilous terrain, the battleground of warring camps of armed ideologues. More dangerous still, any discussion of gender is likely to veer into the chancy and hazardous consideration of sexual object choice. Ever since Stonewall, gay people, having barely survived several generations of researchers and therapists who dismissed them as "freaks of nature"—the dismissal always based on the unstated assumption that homosexuality was an unwelcome abnormality that must be understood in order to be avoided—have rejected the subject of "causality" as a weapon of the enemy, a subjective time bomb likely to explode at the touch.

Yet the subject can't be avoided if we're to get beyond the exchange of pugnacious, militantly shallow views. Besides, sentient human beings will always wonder how we came to be the kind of people we are, and how our bodies and minds interact.

The questions will exist even if we continue to avoid trying to deal with them.

I know of no better way to begin than with Rebecca Jordan-Young's superb book *Brain Storm* (2010). Jordan-Young spent thirteen years analyzing hundreds of studies dating back to 1967, and gathering several thousand individual histories, in order to explore the current state of "brain-organization" research. She starts her book with a question: "How could gayness take a single identifiable form in the brain when it takes such varied forms in people's lives?" The question is aimed directly at Simon LeVay's famous assertion in 1991 that he'd found a difference in brain structure between gay and straight men. His claim was put on the front page of the *New York Times* and from there was trumpeted widely. Multiple hosannas heralded the news that the mystery of sexual orientation had at last been solved. Not only had the existence of "a gay male brain" been established— thereby (whew!) disproving the terrifying suggestion that everyone is capable of a bisexual response—but the source of its differentness had been successfully traced to atypical prenatal hormone exposures.

Jordan-Young looked at some of the studies on which these claims were based, wasn't impressed by the quality of the science, and decided to embark on a comprehensive review of the literature. It wasn't only the claim of "a gay brain" that made her suspicious, but also the number of recent studies that had "found" significant dissimilarities between male and female brains. One that had appeared in 2000, for example, had flatly asserted that the absence of women in science and engineering was due not to bias or socialization but rather to "exposure to testosterone during a key phase of fetal development [that] appears to influence spatial ability and some aspects of personality." This despite the fact that as early as 1974 the psychologists Anke Ehrhardt and Susan Baker had suggested that prenatal hormone effects "in human beings are subtle and can in no way be taken as a basis for prescribing social roles."[35]

In separating the wheat from the chaff, Jordan-Young took on an enormous task. Conclusions from the large assortment of brain studies had landed all over the map. Some neuroscientists had found no clear-cut differences between females and males, others had concluded that some "subtle average" differences did exist, and still others that the differences were "dramatic." As recently as 2006 the neuropsychiatrist Louanne Brizendine claimed in her book *The Female Brain* that the "sex-related centers in the male brain are actually about two times larger than parallel structures in the female brain"—which Jordan-Young authoritatively characterizes as "pure imagination."[36]

Claims have also been made for differences in the corpus callosum (a band of tissue connecting the brain's left and right hemispheres), but biologist Anne Fausto-Sterling's impeccable series of studies found *no* absolute gender difference. Other areas of the brain have also been hailed—to considerable media attention—as *the* site of male-female and gay-straight differences, but with a single exception all efforts to replicate Brizendine's initial claim have failed. The one exception is a difference in volume in a tiny area (the INAH3) of the anterior hypothalamus that *might* be related "to some aspect of sexual function"—but is certainly not responsible for anything significant enough (as LeVay continues to claim) to form "a gay brain." Surely, Jordan-Young concludes, "after more than two centuries of effort ... any 'obvious' differences would have emerged by now." Nor has any significant difference been found in how men and women *use* their brains when engaged in similar tasks—in other words, any disparity in cognitive skills.

It's also long been thought, in regard to an individual's gender identification, that so-called CAH women—prenatal females exposed to unusually high levels of androgen, the signature male hormone—are as adults subject to a high rate of gender dysphoria (that is, changing, or wishing to change, one's assigned gender). Not so, it turns out. Nor has the use of DES (synthetic estrogen) to prevent miscarriages produced any notable distortion—as many studies had predicted—in cognitive abilities such as spatial relations, sex-typed play preferences, or sexual orientation.

None of which has prevented the psychologist Simon Baron-Cohen from publishing a best-selling book, *The Essential Difference: The Truth about the Male and Female Brain,* in which he declares that "the female brain is predominantly hard-wired for empathy [and] the male brain is predominantly hard-wired for understanding and building systems"—a divergence that Baron-Cohen correlates to differing levels of fetal testosterone. Yet in a series of carefully controlled experiments William Byne and his colleagues concluded that "the major expansion of the brain occurs post-natal while the individual is in constant interaction with the environment." The Byne team also concluded that—contra Simon LeVay—the variations in size of INAH3 in the hypothalamus is likely the result of experiences later in life, not (as LeVay would have it) in utero. Jordan-Young's summation of this miasma of contradictory studies is to me persuasive: "Neither prenatal stress, nor neuroendocrine function, nor any somatic characteristics are reliably related to sexual orientation or gender identity."[37]

Still left unanswered, as Jordan-Young acknowledges, are a heap of centrally important issues, including political ones. Is sexual satisfaction more important to men than women? How many sexual partners over how long a period of time is it "normal" to want—or have? Are there real differences in male and female sexual behaviors? If so, what causes them?

Some historical perspective might be useful at this point. During the Renaissance in Europe, women were commonly regarded as sexually insatiable; during the Victorian period, women's interest in sex was said to reside solely in making babies—a woman who enjoyed or pursued sex was thought to have overtaxed her delicate brain with too much reading, and was sent away for a rest cure in the mountains (where her properly passive indifference to sex was purportedly restored). Before 1700 (according to the historian Randolph Trumbach) adult male "rakes" in Europe's large cities had sex with both women and boys, while effeminate "fops" were interested solely in sex with women.[38] As for the standard assumption that men have the stronger sexual appetite, it remains unsupported by physiological evidence (it is women, not men, who are capable of multiple orgasms over a short time span).

You get the picture: what is considered "normal" male or female sexual behavior, and the extent to which the two are said to differ, has varied enormously through time, making it difficult to believe in any biologically predetermined, let alone self-evident, pattern. Which further means that certain hoary "truths" can now be discarded: women *do* masturbate; they *do* fantasize about (and sometimes have) multiple partners; they *don't* associate sex solely with romance; men are *not* naturally more libidinous, aggressive, or initiatory than women, nor are they more interested in pornography, more "ever-ready," more into Kama Sutra "experiments." And, no, the male hormone testosterone neither galvanizes male nor impairs female sexuality. Where male and female sexuality were once—and not long ago—considered sharply different and contrasting, they are more accurately seen as similar (with women potentially the more libidinous of the two).

Nor do prenatal hormones account for the wide disparity often claimed to exist between male and female *non*sexual interests and pursuits. Yes, some differences do exist, but the question is: Are they key aspects of gender, or marginal ones, and in any case, what accounts for them? A major initial problem is that certain attitudes and activities have long been sex-typed as "masculine" or "feminine." Boys, we've long been told, are naturally more vigorous, assertive, and competitive; girls more sedentary, cooperative, emotional, and romantic. Such claims, along with being sexist, reflect outmoded attitudes about gender that are more typical of the Victorian period than our own day. The cultural shifts of the past hundred years have resulted in different values being placed upon different personality traits. A decorative, passive, marriage-oriented female is no longer seen as the ideal model, the one to emulate. Nor is a nonnurturing, emotionally constricted, career-obsessed man any longer widely viewed as "natural" to masculinity.

With declining social pressure to conform to Victorian models of gender destiny, researchers have been revisiting value-laden "findings" from the past. Jordan-Young reports a series of experiments in which "the most *popular* toy with *all* of the girls was a toy long coded as masculine: the Lincoln Logs ... twice as much time was spent with that toy as with any other toy." The second-most popular toy among girls was also masculine-coded: a garage with four cars. The baby doll was the toy *least* appealing to the girls. As more and more such studies accumulate, it becomes increasingly difficult to believe that the traits we've been trained to regard as masculine or feminine are biologically predetermined—due in particular to prenatal hormones.

Thanks largely to the work of feminist researchers, the notion that our traditional sex roles are foreordained has been dethroned, and with it the cramped depiction of men and women as destined to inhabit separate worlds—a view that has for so long constricted our (female *and* male) humanity. There's still a distance to go, but currently women are much more likely to be seen as temperamentally equipped for an expansive set of social roles than they were, say, fifty years ago—with the result that they've become much more prominent in the worlds of higher education, politics, science, medicine, and the law, and much *less* confined to child-rearing and domestic chores. Jordan-Young has put the matter perfectly: "Gender can be re-conceptualized as an 'effect' rather than a mere fact, something that *requires explanation* rather than something that *explains* the social world" (her italics).[39]

Purported gender differences change remarkably when the social environment changes. Higher education is one example. Prior to the countercultural and feminist revolutions of the sixties and seventies, the number of men with bachelor degrees far exceeded the number of women; by 2005 66 percent of graduates in the nation's largest university system (California) were women. Obviously the shift is not due to women undergoing a massive series of testosterone injections, but rather to a radical change in social expectations. None of which is to say that prenatal hormones play no role whatever in gender development, but only that their role has been grossly exaggerated. Even in regard to spatial cognition—one of the few areas where hormonal differences are still thought (though the matter remains contested) to give males, on average, something of an advantage—behavioral intervention, such as encouraging women to watch video games, has produced "substantial gains" in their spatial capacity, all but eliminating the male advantage. In other words, even in the few areas where prenatal hormones do appear to have some effect on postnatal behavior, we're dealing not with hard-wired differences—as is usually claimed—but with plastic, malleable traits.

Has a comparable revolution taken place in how we currently view sexual orientation? It depends greatly on which research you choose to believe and which assumptions you start with (consciously or not) when evaluating the evidence. On close examination, the research often seems based on unexamined presuppositions, which results in murky and contested conclusions about the effect of prenatal hormones on sexual orientation. Among the few matters about which researchers have tended to agree is that sexual orientation is established at an early age, though the particular expressive form it takes ultimately hinges on individual interaction with an ever-changing social environment.

If we move to the next logical question—what are the most accurate criteria for labeling an individual's orientation?—the view fogs over, with the specialists in heated disagreement. Some prefer a behavioral definition (the number of actual sexual contacts or, alternatively, the frequency of sexual fantasies), while others rely on the individual's self-definition, which, depending on the researcher's own frame of reference, can hinge on sexual acts, physical arousal—or feelings of romantic love.

Differ though they often did about which criteria to use when defining the causality of a person's sexual orientation, researchers in the past clustered around our old friends the prenatal hormones. But that unity no longer holds. After a detailed, meticulous scrutiny of "the hormonal question" Jordan-Young concludes, to my mind persuasively, that previous studies have in fact shown that *"extreme cross-sex hormone exposures are associated with only very small shifts in sexual orientation* ... the data aren't just weak, they are broadly contradictory" (Jordan-Young's emphasis).[40]

In regard both to gender and sexual orientation, the simple dichotomies of the past—male *or* female, gay *or* straight—have proven woefully inadequate for dealing with an explosion in the way people are now choosing to define themselves. The torrent of information from anthropological studies alone has for some time been dealing "Western reality" a body blow. We now know that some non-Western societies have long recognized three or more genders, including the *hijra* of India, the *xanith* of Oman, the two-spirited Native American berdache, the Kathoey of Thailand, the Mahu of Hawaii, and the *fa'afafine* of Polynesia—among others. There's been a comparable floodtide of information, historical as well as anthropological, documenting the deeply embedded, widespread incidence of homosexuality through time and across the globe.

How well has the scientific community—our alternative priesthood—reacted to this massive accumulation of challenging new evidence? Not well. Mostly, they ignore it, consumed by their own current research and (like the rest of us) irritated at the prospect of having to rethink what they'd been taught was unimpeachable truth. What professional researchers and ordinary common folk share is an entrenched reluctance to consider what connection if any exists between gender nonconformity and homosexuality. "Homonormative" gay people have long reacted as if to a bee sting to any attempt at connecting them to gender "outlaws" like transsexuals, drag queens, or trans people.

Yes, the *T* in LGBTQ does refer to "trans," and the national gay organizations do now and then feint in the direction of representing its own "renegades"—but it ain't with a smile or with much largesse.

One common attitude among normative gays—though under pressure and increasingly disguised—is that trans people are simply "wrong" about themselves. They're said to suffer from a mental disorder, mistakenly equating a passing identification with the opposite gender with a biological imperative—a mistake they would outgrow if they'd learn to be patient *and* learn to embrace their gay sexual orientation. The basis for that attitude, I suspect, may well be an unconscious wish in normative circles to win certification *for themselves* as traditional men (rough, tough) or women (delicate, decorous)—even while knowing that such outmoded notions of masculinity and femininity are fatuous and false. The opposite argument, ironically—the one that fully accepts the reality of the transgender experience—is the one that has helped to *disrupt* what until recently has been the longstanding equation of gender variance with homosexuality.

David Valentine, in his stimulating book *Imagining Transgender: An Ethnography of a Category,* has further complicated the picture. It turns out that a significant number of the participants in his study labeled as transgender by social service agencies in fact self-describe as gay, thereby once again *recombining* (and confusing) gender identity with sexual orientation.[41] Valentine's book is, to be sure, ten years old; in the years since his study, the term *transgender* has gotten far wider usage, and there's a real possibility that any number of his informants would today refer to themselves as trans—not gay.

Still, Valentine raises an important issue regarding terminology. To use *transgender* as a category of analysis, he argues, is by implication to ascribe all prejudice leveled at a given individual to their gender variance—thereby eliding other kinds of social discrimination, like those based on race, class, cultural background, and even one's location in regard to global economics. Social scientists and activists have come to describe the juncture of these overlapping categories as "intersectionality," which, it's argued, more broadly (and more accurately) accounts for the panoply of discriminations that confront certain individuals. Valentine goes still further: while recognizing the progressive intent behind the use of *transgender* as a category, he argues that in practice it "actually reproduces, in novel and intensified forms, class and racial hierarchies."

Ever since *transgender* came into common use in the mid-1990s as an umbrella term, the ground has continued to shift as to what kinds of person the term did (or should) encompass. Should it logically include male transvestites, even though the majority of cross-dressers are heterosexual in orientation? What about "drag queens" who perform publicly as female impersonators, unlike heterosexual transvestites who *privately* wear clothes traditionally associated with the "opposite" sex, and may or may not do so for erotic gratification? Should "butch" lesbians or "effeminate" gay men be included in the transgender category? And what about "drag kings," some of whom perform as male impersonators, while others always dress in "male" clothing but do not perform publicly? Gender variance, in sum, comes in various forms, and those included under the "transgender" umbrella vary according to an individual's self-definition as well as to an outside observer's chosen terminology.

As Valentine notes, "These definitional issues have political effects." The middle-class members of the pre-Stonewall Mattachine Society and the Daughters of Bilitis, for example,

rejected (in the case of Mattachine) the radical class consciousness of the group's communist founders. Members of both
homophile groups emphasized a model of homosexuality that
conformed to a gender-normative outer self-presentation that
(in the Daughters of Bilitis) proved unwelcoming to working-
class butch lesbians. GLF and GAA did somewhat better in the
years immediately following the Stonewall riots in challenging
traditional "maleness" and "femaleness," but not better enough
to avoid the famous incident in the early seventies when the
gender radical Sylvia Rivera was booed off the stage of the Gay
Pride rally—and thereafter resigned from the movement.

To complicate matters further, many of the cross-dressing
gay men who today attend the lavish annual Night of a Thousand Gowns are adamant in rejecting any identification with the
trans community. Nor do these white, middle- and upper-class
gay men see themselves as having much of anything in common
with the young and poor African American and Latino "queens"
who support themselves, in drag, as sex workers. David Valentine sums up the complexity of the issues relating to gender
identity when reporting on his interviews with "Anita." She
claims several identities—including gay and drag queen—but
does not claim, despite taking hormones and living as a woman,
that she is either trans or female. Yet at one point she tells Valentine, "I don't wanna go back to a man, you know."

Anita, like many of Valentine's interviewees, "is hard-pressed
to align her self-understanding with discrete categories of identity," like "woman," "gay," "transvestite," or "transgender." The
implication is that she is no longer a man, yet not a woman, and
Valentine stresses "the instabilities of the category transgender
when applied to individual lives." All of which raises a troubling
question: Are the gender categories with which we nontrans-

sexuals confidently assign ourselves any less unstable? The growing appeal of "gender fluidity," especially among the young, may well reflect a gender-queer perspective that leaves standard categories of male and female further in the dust—even as trans people continue, it appears, to police their borders with greater stringency.

In Valentine's view "the increasing institutional power of transgender to order certain experiences ... [in the process] erases their complexity." He encourages us to see that perhaps the core problem with the mainstream LGBTQ national movement is that its adherents suppress the actual intricacy of lived experience, downplaying the frequency with which our lives fail to slip easily into established, middle-class identity categories. From that perspective "Gay Pride" translates into the false assumption that the categories we employ to describe ourselves are accurate, stable reflections of our experience and, further, that their rigid usage removes from consideration the host of incoherent impulses and maverick fantasies that separate individuals—not to mention the barrier it creates to expressing class and racial subcultural variations. We're deceived into believing that labels like *gay* are something more than towers of sand. In truth we—all of us—are profoundly *weird* or, to use the latest, more universalizing category, profoundly *queer*.

Other kinds of objections have been made concerning the credibility of transgender (or "gay" or "straight") identities—objections that, unlike those of David Valentine, are often raised by those who, shedding a profusion of crocodile tears, declare profound sympathy for the plight of those suffering from what they call gender dysphoria. A typical example is the position taken by Professor of Clinical Psychiatry Richard A. Friedman in his 2015 *New York Times* article "How Changeable Is Gender?"[42]

Friedman comes out strongly in the article against surgical treatment to change one's body to "fit" one's psychological conviction of gender identity. The outcomes for such surgery, he argues, are "suboptimal." In support of that conclusion Friedman cites (as do many opponents of transgender surgery) a Swedish study that found no reduction in depression or suicide: 41 percent of trans people in the study attempted suicide at some point after sex reassignment surgery, compared with 4.6 percent of the general public. What Friedman fails to mention, as his critics have been quick to point out, is that the study's control group was recruited not from transgender people who hadn't had surgery, but rather from the cisgender general population. For those who transitioned after 1989, moreover—as attitudes toward gender nonconformity grew more accepting—the suicide rate was much closer to that of the general population.[43]

Friedman is also either unaware of or chooses to ignore a variety of reports that have reached quite different conclusions. Virtually every contemporary study has found that less than 2 percent of transgender people undergoing surgery subsequently regret their decision—and even then, the grounds for regret center on the results of the surgery itself or on the ongoing social disapproval they continue to experience. Nor is it true, as a frequently cited Danish study has claimed, that *without* surgery 80 percent of gender-nonconforming children grow out of their discomfort with their own bodies. Proponents of alternative behavior modification therapy—most prominently Kenneth Zucker—hailed the study as proving the lack of necessity for surgery. But in fact the study is unreliable. It fails to distinguish between the gender-nonconforming tomboy and the intensely unhappy female child whose insistence that she is male persists throughout adolescence.[44]

As for the cause of transgenderism, the studies of researchers and the claims of activists run all over the map—just as they do in regard to sexual orientation, and with equally inconclusive results. For one, Georg S. Kranz at the Medical University of Vienna reported in a 2014 study what he claimed were structural differences in the brains of trans people (here we go again). Using a high-resolution technique called diffusion tensor imaging to measure something called "mean diffusivity," Kranz has found a distinctive neural signature for trans people. Yet Kranz's findings need not only replication before they can be granted any authority, but also interpretation (the possibility, for example, that environmental and behavioral factors may have produced the differential patterns within the brain).

Yet another area of controversy surrounds the comparatively recent use (it was first approved in 1989) of the gonadotropin-releasing hormone analogue (GnRH) after puberty has started to block and delay the development of secondary sex characteristics. To date the benefits seem considerable, though the protocol is still controversial. As the clinical professor of psychiatry Vernon Rosario has put it, "Even experts wonder: how stable is transgender identification in a teenager? Could the treatment itself (for psychological or neurological reasons) reinforce trans identity? What could be the long-term health effects?" What *is* unquestionably true, I believe, is that the use of GnRH does contribute to a considerable increase in a sense of well-being among "gender dysphoric" adolescents. GnRH also makes it far more likely that the decision-making process about surgery will land directly in the hands of the adolescents themselves rather than being left to their parents or their doctors, as will how they prefer to define themselves—some have chosen "gender-queer" or "no gender" rather than "transgender." Until recently an *intersexed* (mixed genitalia) baby would, on the all but unanimous advice of the medical community, be rushed into an irreversible either-or (binary male or female) surgical change *before* a conscious gender identity could become manifest—yet to this day surgical intervention in infancy remains a common "treatment."[45]

In regard to the "cause" of sexual orientation, the recent scientific discussion has been conflicted, repetitious, and problematic. Yet it can't be avoided, though the official gay movement has done its best to announce the subject closed. The Human Rights Campaign has issued a literal edict: homosexuality is inborn; no element of choice is involved other than how one decides to create from that biologically determined fact a particular lifestyle. Younger activists seem to find the longstanding debate over etiology both boring and trivial. They apparently view scientific inquiry—which long championed a pathological view of homosexuality and made life for gay people miserable—as forever doomed to remain little more than a cunning disguise for prejudice.

It's my impressionistic sense that many of the radical young implicitly share HRC's assumption that they've had no choice in "deciding" their sexual orientation—that *some* sort of genetic or hormonal predisposition, apparently unrecoverable, was at play. They don't much care, one way or the other; as Pink Tank, a group of queer activists in New York City, has succinctly put it, "We don't have to figure out why we are queer. It doesn't matter." They avoid the conundrum of *how* they became "that way" and focus instead on what they should do about it—how they should choose to lead their lives. The radical young simply accept their differentness, or claim to, see no reason to explain or apologize for it, and go on doing the world's work.[46]

I'm partly in sympathy with that stance. My own recent attempt to read through the "scientific" literature on homosexuality, or even a portion of it, has been a dreary exercise, a scholastic version of masochism. Yet the recondite chore still seems a necessary one: the position that scientific inquiry takes, or that—since its conclusions are currently garbled and inconclusive—the public *thinks* it has taken, on the question of why some people are sexually queer or gender-queer has profound consequences for how the rest of the populace views us, and how we view ourselves. It deeply affects our quality of life.

A case in point is the "reparative therapy" that the recently deceased Joseph Nicolosi and his cohorts have been pushing for some time; homosexuality, in reparative circles, is not explained by biology but rather by childhood trauma exacerbated by a particular family configuration (dominant mother, detached father)—a theory that harkens back to the psychoanalytic views associated with Irving Bieber and Charles Socarides that dominated the professional discourse in the 1950s and '60s. Nicolosi claims that he's "cured" about a third of his patients.

The political stakes in this debate are high, and not to engage in it leaves the field to the homophobes. At the present moment the public is evenly split on the contest between biology and environment. Over the past four decades the view has steadily gained ground—rising from about 12 percent in 1977 to 42 percent in 2014—that some people are simply born gay or lesbian. A Pew Research Center poll in 2013 showed that exactly the same number of Americans—42 percent—believe that being gay "is just the way some choose to live."[47]

One way of understanding the current spectrum of opinion on causality is to start with a close look at a recent, fifty-six-page article in the prestigious journal *Psychological Science*. Coauthored by six of the best-known specialists in the field (including J. Michael Bailey, the lead author) and entitled "Sexual Orientation, Controversy, and Science," the article is designed to summarize and evaluate the evidence to date. The authors make a strenuous show of objectivity—meaning, they employ scientific language to the hilt—but since objectivity is elusive, their underlying bias does seep through the deceptively dispassionate vocabulary. They do have the grace, though, to remind us constantly that the meaning of this or that phenomenon is "unclear" and the research "scant," "not replicated," or "not decisive."[48]

They start off well enough: "The possibility that people differ in sexual orientation because of hormonal differences," they write, "has been the most influential causal hypothesis involving a specific mechanism ... [yet] there is little direct evidence for this hypothesis." Which isn't to say, they go on, that hormones have no effect on our *physical* sex differences, and in particular our internal and external sex organs (though the authors find "no conclusive evidence that homosexual and heterosexual people differ in their genital anatomy"). They proceed to weigh the evidence from studies of atypical prenatal exposure to the male hormone androgen, and conclude that they are full of "important limitations." Even so, they refuse to abandon the theory, on the grounds that "good hypotheses are difficult to test"—an instance where their subjectivity directly surfaces, since they persist in calling a hypothesis good even though they themselves have found insufficient evidence to confirm it.

"If hormones are not the persuasive agents of sexual orientation," they go on to ask, can we perhaps evoke "genes" as an explanatory tool? "The lure of the gay gene" (as Ryan Conrad entitled his impressive summary of the issue) has a long history.

The notion of a gay gene was once at the heart of a protracted and heated debate between "essentialists" and "social constructionists"—though it no longer, as Conrad puts it, "preoccupies the queer political imagination" (not that any other theory has taken its place). Yet aspects of the debate do continue to resonate in scientific quarters.

Twin studies are a case in point. Franz Kallmann, back in the 1940s and '50s, found in his studies of forty pairs of monozygotic (identical) twins and forty-five pairs of dizygotic (fraternal) twins, a higher rate of homosexuality among the former—that is, among those siblings whose genes are entirely shared. Kallmann concluded that homosexuality was an inherited trait, and his finding was replicated some thirty years later by a British research team; by Richard Pillard, a professor of psychiatry, in 1991 in a study that included women and nontwin siblings; and by J. Michael Bailey (yes, *that* Bailey, lead author of the long 2016 article in *Psychological Science* under discussion).[49]

All three studies, when closely scrutinized by other scientists, have been criticized for assorted sampling inadequacies. The most devastating critique has come from two other specialists, William Byne and Bruce Parsons, and centers on the remarkable fact that concordance rates for homosexuality in nontwin biological brothers (9.2%) and genetically unrelated adoptive brothers (11%) were similar rather than—if a genetic hypothesis for homosexuality were true—higher for the biological siblings. Still more problematic, according to Byne and Parsons, is the fact that a significant number of *identical* twins were discordant for homosexuality—though they not only duplicated each other's genes but were brought up in a similar family environment as well (parental impact on different children in the same family, of course, is never *exactly* the same).

Comparable claims and counterclaims have afflicted the experimental findings of another notable geneticist, Dean Hamer, as well as the ongoing experiments of the neuroendocrinologist Simon LeVay. Hamer reported in the early 1990s a genetic marker on the Xq28 region of the X chromosome that was present more often in gay than straight men. Hamer did not claim that homosexuality was (like, say, eye color) "inherited" or that the Xq28 marker simply "explained" a homosexual orientation. Even so, with a single recent exception, there have been no successful replications of his findings. LeVay, in turn, has himself—without entirely giving up the game—concluded that genetic studies have been inconclusive and that "multiple factors"—neither named nor prioritized—explain sexual orientation.[50]

A number of still-later analyses have roundly criticized the inadequate conceptual models and research designs of the studies purporting to have discovered genetic links to sexual orientation, and have together concluded that all theories regarding the existence of a "gay gene" are unsubstantiated. The Bailey team's judgment in their lengthy *Psychological Science* summary is less absolute. With a good bit of suspect hemming and hawing about sampling biases and the like, they nonetheless come down on the side—their "best estimate"—of genetic factors playing a "moderate—certainly not overwhelming"—role. "Is sexual orientation genetic?" they ask; and their answer is as evasive as their question is concrete: "Probably somewhat genetic, but not mostly so"—which gives pussyfooting a whole new dimension. In contrast, they immediately follow with the statement, startlingly firm, that "the evidence for environmental influence is unequivocal." That same conclusion—to which the Human Rights Campaign will not take kindly—has been reached by a number of other researchers; they stress, and even more assertively than the Bailey team, that environmental factors are the primary components in the formation of sexual orientation.

The question then becomes: *Which* environmental factors? Here the leading candidate, according to the Bailey team, is unquestionably "developmental factors in early childhood," with parental behavior singled out as the most important such factor. Bailey et al. elaborate: "To the extent that a trait is not genetic, it is caused by the environment, not by free will." If a trait is not present from birth, then it is the product of events occurring after birth; environmental factors, it should be noted, are also impersonal forces impervious to choice. We are, in short, devoid of agency. No matter which side of the argument you take, genetics or environment, human decision making is an irrelevance. The sole choice available to us is abstinence; we play no role in establishing our basic orientation other than deciding not to indulge it (a decision, one could further argue, itself predetermined by forces beyond our awareness).

A host of questions surround the decision to implicate the "environment" in producing sexual orientation. What do we make of the fact that genetically identical twins often diverge in their sexual orientation—despite their identical genetic makeup and their (mostly) comparable family environment? What accounts for their landing in different sexual zones? Could it be that parents treat each of their children *very* differently, that "family culture" is not a force consistently applied, but rather changes shape and emphasis through time, its decrees and prescriptions applied in constantly varying ways? Still further: When the experts tell us that family culture plays a formative role in the development of sexual orientation, how can we be sure that what's crucially at play aren't underlying genetic factors asserting themselves *despite* an essentially unwelcoming social environment—though not one antithetical enough to alter the trajectory?

The most prominent theory regarding the effect of "pathological" parent-child relationships is also the longest-lived. In 1962 Irving Bieber's team of researchers published *Homosexuality: A Psychoanalytical Study,* which claimed a close-binding, intimate mother in combination with a detached or hostile father is responsible for a son's homosexuality (by implication, the reverse configuration—a close-binding father and a detached mother—accounts for a daughter's lesbianism). UCLA professor Evelyn Hooker mounted the first substantive challenge to the Bieber study; she pointed to the fact that its subjects were all undergoing psychiatric treatment, making them unreliable representatives of the larger gay male community. Yet a 1969 study based on *non*patient homosexual males confirmed Bieber's findings in the partial sense of finding a correlation between "troubled" parental relationships and gay children. Several other studies have affirmed a linkage between a poor father-son relationship and a homosexual outcome for the son.

More recently, the psychiatrist Richard Isay proposed a variation on the "parental theory" that shifted the paradigm: a young son who persists in gender-atypical behavior, Isay argued, can alienate a traditional-minded father. Yet as with so many of the studies that preceded his, Isay failed to explain the *internal* psychoanalytic mechanism that a father's disdain sets off in the boy, and which then leads to a homosexual outcome. Does it have to do with a failure on the son's part, because of his father's indifference or hostility, to "identify" with maleness? Or does the homosexual outcome represent the need to find—to capture the interest and regard—of a substitute male figure? And why would either scenario necessarily produce *sexual* lust and *physical* sexual contact?

Conundrum is piled upon conundrum—though far too many of the experts seem unaware of or uninterested in the intricate issues their own research has raised. And none of them deal with a question that Kinsey long ago posed: instead of focusing on "explaining" what they consider the "anomaly" of same-sex attraction, why not simply accept it as an entirely natural potential in *everyone's* make-up? To start with that assumption would be to pose a very different central question: Why are some people *exclusively* attracted only to those of the same or opposite sex?

Exclusivity, in other words, could be viewed (as it currently isn't) as itself the problematic condition, as symptomatic of a rigid denial, a fearful suppression, of what is an inherent aspect of our constitutional makeup. Scientific researchers would then be investigating why Western culture has sharply diverged from a pattern of bisexual attraction often manifested elsewhere in the world. Instead of trying to understand why some people choose to engage in same-sex relations, they might shift to exploring questions like, Why do those who are rigidly heterosexual turn out to be much more politically conservative—more sexist, racist, classist, and gender-rigid—than those who are not exclusively straight?[51]

Instead of exchanging hot-headed arguments in the scientific journals on the "causes" of homosexual behavior—arcane, inconclusive debates about "the effect of fraternal-birth-order," "finger length ratios," the "maternal immune hypothesis," or the "epigenetic" study of how genes turn on or off—scientists might question their own implacable fixation on an issue that seems to have ended up baffling several generations of researchers.

As scientists continue to pursue the enigma of who lands where on the Kinsey scale and why, one group remains focused on parent-child relationships as centrally implicated in the causal question, while another continues to believe that the answer to the puzzle lies with genetic and hormonal studies. Neither group has made its case, with both arguing from inconclusive, contested evidence. The prestigious Bailey team, in its own lengthy report, seems to fall somewhere in the murky middle. It concludes that genetic and hormonal factors *may* play "a moderate—[but] certainly not overwhelming"—role, yet at the same time declares at one point that "developmental factors in early childhood" form the most promising area for exploring causality. Clouding the picture still further, the report then proceeds to reject the hypothesis that parent-child relationships have a significant effect on sexual orientation, calling this a view with "little scientific promise."

Like Alice in Wonderland, we've fallen down a rabbit hole. But we need to climb out of it, and fast. The *political* ramifications of the debate are serious, and we can't simply wish them away. Waiting in the wings is a group of researchers with impressive scientific qualifications, headed by Paul R. McHugh, who claim to have successfully resolved crucial aspects of the etiological puzzle—and are eager to outline the public policies that should follow in train. In August 2016 McHugh and the biostatistician Lawrence Mayer published a 143-page review of the literature on sexual orientation in the *New Atlantis,* a journal put out by the Ethics and Public Policy Center, a conservative advocacy group. The report wasn't peer-reviewed and contains no original research, yet it has quickly gained traction in the media and been translated into French, German, Arabic, Spanish, and Russian. The report isn't a mere rant: McHugh and his associates do acknowledge that sexual identity can sometimes be fluid, and that there's still a great deal that we don't understand about the origins of sexual orientation.[52]

Having made that bow to modesty, the McHugh report proceeds to declare categorically that no evidence exists in regard to
transgender identity for the claim that either puberty blockers
for adolescents or surgery for adults is safe or effectively improves
life for those undergoing treatment. The report also insists that
the higher rate of mental illness in the LGBTQ community is *not*
the result, even in part, of social stigma. Mental disorder,
McHugh implies, is *intrinsic* to being gay or transgender. Both
conditions are *chosen* and therefore subject to corrective treatment. To its credit, the Human Rights Campaign—which is
wedded to the theory that homosexuality is hard-wired—has
launched a website, *McHugh Exposed*, to counteract his views. Yet
they continue to spread. What it comes down to—with scientists
at odds with each other—is who you choose to believe: transgender people themselves who insist that hormones and surgery
have improved their lives, or the "McHugh scientists," who discount such testimony as delusionary, the product of underlying
illness.

The debate over causality isn't going away, and the gay and
transgender communities can no longer afford to ignore or dismiss it. The political consequences are too grave.

IV

Whose Left?

The national gay movement's recent absorption in the right to marry has focused our energy on a goal—the loving couple, the tight-knit family—that positions the movement squarely within the framework of a Norman Rockwell painting—the one already on its way to the attic. As the bridal parties continue their stampede to the altar, they seem not to have noticed that nonbelievers are burning down the church. If forced to choose, those of us on the Left would probably opt for the infidels.

It's no longer the case—as it was back in 1970 with the Gay Liberation Front—that the national gay movement can claim to represent any position situated even one inch left of center—or that it wants to be. For that matter, it's not clear whether there's a coherent Left to be part of, to what extent its programmatic goals align with those of the LGBTQ movement's left wing, or whether in any case the straight left gives a damn.

Many of the issues that currently define and dominate left-wing politics in general—making higher education free, raising the minimum wage, reforming the criminal justice system, reversing climate change, addressing the predations of globalization, repairing the infrastructure, taxing the wealthy, guaranteeing an annual income—are surely not central or even, in most instances, peripheral to the agenda of the gay movement's national organizations. Its tactics, goals, and ambitions are simply those of a typical ethnic group, hell-bent on getting inside the machine, and careful not to throw even a small wrench in the gears.

The most conservative of the national gay organizations, the Human Rights Campaign, having captured the crown of legal marriage, has shifted its priorities not to a more inclusive support for the goals of the Left in general, but rather to getting federal legislation passed to end all remaining forms of discrimination against gay people. That goal is indisputably worthy— and just as indisputably insular. HRC's focus remains entirely inward; like a blinded mole, it has burrowed still deeper into the tunnel of *self*-protection—and the rest of the world (including the low-income gay world) be damned.

HRC *has* recently been speaking out against the spread of anti-trans "bathroom bills"—despite an abysmal earlier record on trans rights—yet at the same time has elevated Caitlin Jenner to its ranks of "Celebrity Supporters," though her parodic attempts at replicating pre-feminist "femininity" has few supporters in the trans community—not to mention the feminist movement. In 2016 HRC endorsed Republican senator Mark Kirk of Illinois in his successful reelection campaign over his challenger, Democratic representative Tammy Duckworth. Kirk had scored only a 78 out of 100 on HRC's own score card, in comparison to Duckworth's 100, but the organization nonetheless attempted to justify its endorsement on the grounds that Kirk had come out in support of the "Equality Act," HRC's suggested federal antidiscrimination bill, and in the conviction that sympathetic Republicans should be rewarded when sticking their necks out. HRC prides itself on its sophistication in playing "the long game."[1]

It shouldn't. It has opted for an appallingly short-sighted strategy. The only way the "Equality Act" will ever be passed by the

U.S. Senate is if the Democrats regain control of Congress. HRC president Chad Griffin defended the support of Kirk by saying he's "a strong ally in the Republican Party," but that was way overstating the case; Kirk was nobody's idea of a progressive—and Tammy Duckworth most definitely was. As Michelangelo Signorile wrote on Twitter, HRC as recently as 2014 "was still supporting the narrow Employment Non-discrimination Act" [ENDA] with its appalling exemption for "religious conscience," while every other national LGBTQ group—except the Log Cabin Republicans—had joined the twenty-first century and pulled its support.[2]

In contrast to HRC, the younger generation of radical gay local organizations is focused on survival issues—like how to provide for homeless youth, how to combat brutal deportation policies and an inhumane criminal justice system, and how to cope with violence against trans people. To them, devoting energy to pie-in-the-sky lobbying for repairs to our infrastructure is comparable to petitioning for free lessons in Mandarin. Their primary concern is with the *least* privileged members of the LGBTQ community, the people most desperately in need of help. And the need is great.

Though the common perception is that gay people are affluent—the *Will & Grace* stereotype, reinforced by high-income celebrities who have come out in the past few years—a recent report on hunger in the United States found that more than one in four of the twenty thousand lesbian and gay adults surveyed had at least once in the past year been unable to feed themselves or their families, compared to one in six heterosexual adults. (Had trans people and homeless LGBTQ teenagers been included in the study, the story would have been more dire still.) Four years ago, another report found that gay people also had high rates of job discrimination and low rates of health insurance. For nonwhite gays, the figures are still worse. Nearly half of gay African Americans have experienced hunger over the past year (compared with 28 percent of heterosexual African Americans), and the comparable figures for gay Hispanics are 33 percent (24 percent for those who are straight).[3]

Unlike the middle- and upper-class gay people who seem content with HRC's single-issue politics, the youthful radicals at work on the grassroots level *are* attuned to many of the issues that currently dominate the straight left's agenda. The members of Southerners on New Ground (SONG) and the legions of the young who worked for Bernie Sanders share much in common, including an awareness of the pervasive divisions of class never clearly articulated in national politics. Yet it would be a mistake simply to view Bernie's troops and the radical young gays who make up groups like SONG as natural soul mates. They're more like *potential* allies, and whether or not they end up working closely together, it seems to me, hinges on how far the Bernie-ites move in the direction of SONG, rather than vice-versa. Sanders has adopted the label "democratic socialist," but he's in fact ideologically closer (as Sanders has himself acknowledged) to FDR and the New Deal—and all but oblivious (unlike at least *some* of his followers) to the sex-gender revolution central to the radical gay vanguard.[4]

Sanders's main enemy is economic inequality and the self-satisfied profiteers who sit atop the pyramid, which puts him in the long line of progressive liberals. He declares himself firmly anticapitalist, yet what this has generally boiled down to is a staunch demand for a $15 minimum wage. Sanders doesn't talk about "redistributing" the wealth through higher tax rates on the rich or placing a ceiling on executive pay. Nor has he spoken out in support of Elizabeth Warren's fervent call for a new social contract under which "all workers ... should have some basic protections and be able to build some economic security for themselves and their families."[5]

Similarly, Sanders's feminism seems more in line with Betty Friedan than Shulamith Firestone, and his advocacy of gay rights is more in tune with the nondiscrimination goals of the Human Rights Campaign than with the trans revolution's depth-charge challenge to the traditional gender binary. The same is true of other prominent left formations that have recently arisen—the Working Families Party, the National People's Action, the Dream Defenders, and Black Lives Matter. Their concentration on the inequities of our current system importantly addresses economic inequality and racism, along with somewhat inchoate references now and then to the rigid barriers of class.

But working to adjust the maldistribution of income and to end racism doesn't constitute an agenda broad enough to encompass either the sex-gender revolution that young gay radicals are spearheading or the root-and-branch opposition to capitalism exemplified by the (mostly straight) radicals who have coalesced around the journal *Jacobin*. Perhaps I can best illustrate the gap between these two groups on the one hand and the Bernie Sanders progressives on the other with reference to an essay I wrote long ago about the Cuban revolution. After praising the revolution's accomplishments in improving the material conditions of life for the average Cuban, I suggested that those gains might be regarded as the starting point rather than the final resting place for what the revolution might still attain. I located that future place "in the area of psychosexual transformation ... in which 'male' and 'female' have become outmoded differentiations."[6]

I was well aware, I added, that in arguing for this "new vision when most of the world still goes to bed hungry at night" could be regarded as "a luxury and an illusion, the decadent yearning of a society already sated with possessions—but not with the satisfactions they were supposed to have brought in train.... For the vast majority of people in the world," I acknowledged, "the 'older' vision of freedom from material want is still so distantly utopian that perhaps only a citizen of the United States could be provincial enough to doubt its continuing centrality."

Forty-five years later, the "new vision" remains remote, but the distance to it has somewhat narrowed. For the radicals of *Jacobin,* the path forward is along the well-trodden Marxist path of abolishing capitalism and private property—a goal well beyond the horizons of a Bernie Sanders. For the sex radicals and trans people of SONG, material want is very much an everyday concern, yet ending it is, for at least some of them, a way station, not a terminal; the long-range vision is psychosocial *as well as* economic.

This makes for a certain amount of common ground with the *Jacobin* stalwarts, but the differences are not petty. The radical gay left is not centrally concerned with ending capitalism, and the *Jacobins,* for their part, don't seem notably concerned with the gender binary nor with the continuing hold of majoritarian values that locate the optimal source of human connectedness and contentment in the monogamous couple and the traditional nuclear family. This isn't to say that either group is oblivious to the primary concerns of the other—unconvinced of their urgency might be closer to the mark.

In this regard the Jacobinites have the edge. In a recent anthology of some dozen essays that Bhaskar Sunkara, the founding editor of *Jacobin,* and Sarah Leonard, a senior editor at

The Nation, recently put together, two are fully, and several others partially, concerned with issues directly related to sexuality and gender. Both essays, moreover—the one by Sarah Leonard and the other by Kate Redburn, a PhD candidate at Yale—are provocative and well informed. Leonard's piece focuses on the ways in which the traditional heterosexual family continues to oppress women. She dismisses the "maternal instinct" as "largely a bogus concept" and, further, deplores the fact that many working-class women are forced to hire themselves out, often at low wages, to ease the domestic burdens of middle-class mothers.[7]

Kate Redburn's essay, "After Gay Marriage," centers on the insufficient attention the national LGBTQ organizations are paying to the needs of the least-prosperous members of the gay community. She particularly emphasizes the plight of many transgender people, who are twice as likely to live in extreme poverty than are cisgender Americans, and she underscores, too, the racialization of queer poverty, with African American gay male couples six times more likely to be poor than their white counterparts. She deplores the way in which the mainstream gay organizations have prioritized civil rights issues and largely ignored social justice ones—"the needs of homeless youth, isolated elders, low-income, and immigrant LGBT people."

To those of us on the Left, Redburn's charge that the national LGBTQ organizations are currently short-changing the least-privileged members of their own community seems wholly justified. Yet, when the grousing expands, as it often does, into minimizing the importance of working for a civil liberties agenda, I think it goes too far. Though I agree that the agendas of HRC and other mainstream gay organizations need expanding, I also think it's important to acknowledge their accomplishments to date—which may prove to have been a necessary prelude to a more expansive mission. Through lobbying, electoral politics, court rulings, and legislation, the national LGBTQ organizations have significantly softened the harsh discriminatory conditions under which gay people have until recently lived.

No one, moreover, should regard even that restricted mission as having now been completed. The conditions under which gay people continue to suffer in much of the world are gruesome; in April 2017, for example, it came to light that in Chechnya gay men were being tortured to death, though in an HBO interview the Chechnyan leader Ramzan Kadyrov denied that gay people existed in his country; if any *were* somehow discovered, Kadyrov said, he would order them deported to Canada in order "to purify our blood." The International Lesbian and Gay Association (ILGA), formed in 1978, works hard to protect sexual minorities around the globe, but finds few supporters among self-absorbed, provincial Americans.[8]

Even in the more "enlightened" countries, homophobia remains alive and well. A 2015 Harris poll showed that in our own, comparatively liberal land a significant amount of entrenched hostility toward gay people remains; fully a third of heterosexuals polled expressed discomfort with the prospect of attending a gay wedding—and, remarkably, of learning that their doctor is gay.

There's still a great deal of work that needs to be done even in the "vanguard" United States to change hearts and minds. What's objectionable about the Human Rights Campaign is not that it works to achieve full protection and citizenship for gay people, but that it seems to care a lot more about those already privileged than about those suffering at a basic level from economic deprivation. Following recent "victories" with regard to marrying and on serving in the military, HRC's agenda has broadened to combat discrimination in the workplace and elsewhere, yet the country's core economic inequalities remain beyond its scope.

In May 2017, HRC announced that it had joined its efforts to those of the preexisting Family Equality Council (originating among a group of gay fathers in 1979, FEC was earlier known as Family Pride) in pushing for the sort of "comprehensive LGBTQ rights bill our families have been waiting for." "Our families"? That's a chilling phrase. Not only does it exclude single people (unless they're parenting), but it makes no mention of outreach to any of the more innovative family structures that have been proliferating across the country—from cohabiting siblings and elders, to polyamorous folks, to communal arrangements of varying sorts. HRC's literature suggests a particular emphasis on adoption rights, a phenomenon pretty much confined to people who can afford to add children to their families—as opposed to poor families who are struggling to feed those they already have. Elsewhere in its literature, HRC describes another of its programs: Triumph through Faith, which looks to religion "as a source of guidance and inspiration." When I read that, the earlier chill in my bones settled instantly into perma-freeze.[9]

While HRC is busy protecting the same traditional families that the Gay Liberation Front was busy deriding fifty years ago, there remain a host of life-threatening national and international issues that all the mainstream gay organizations, not simply HRC, continue to ignore or pay lip service to. There's a hideous amount of injustice in the world that needs to be addressed by us all, whether or not it directly relates to our sexual orientation. If that sounds too highfalutin and moralistic, then we should engage simply for pragmatic reasons: the gay community needs allies and it's only on the Left that we have any real chance of finding them. That means we need to show up for their issues if we expect them to show up for ours.

During the fifteen years that the AIDS epidemic raged uncontrollably through the gay world, its all-consuming horror inescapably monopolized attention. Yet even during the Reagan years, at least one of the larger gay organizations, the National Gay and Lesbian Task Force, *did* show an awareness of the need for "intersectional" work on the grassroots level. NGLTF's board issued a statement in 1991 opposing the Gulf War, and its Policy Institute (under the leadership of John D'Emilio) spoke out in a number of position papers on the issues of affirmative action, welfare reform, and immigration restriction. As D'Emilio has put it, gay activists "who thought of themselves as leftists worked consistently to magnify the movement's lens so that segments of the movement at least stood for a vision of social justice broader than a single-issue politics contained within a civil rights framework."[10]

Yet by the late 1990s a sea change had taken place. The Human Rights Campaign Fund and the Fellowship of (gay) Metropolitan Community Churches together moved to the forefront of the movement and saw to it that the fourth national march for gay rights in 2000 focused on the centrist themes of "faith and family." The movement has ever since nestled comfortably in the lap of mainstream patriotism. Yet on the level of day-to-day political maneuvering, the modus operandi remains tit for tat. Ideally (from my point of view), LGBTQ people and their organizations would become vocal about issues relating to racism, a guaranteed annual income, universal child care and parental leave, prison reform, immigration policy, and the like because they believed those causes are just. True, no one can do it all, but you *can* send in a check or pick up the phone. There are many ways to participate actively while still leaving enough time and energy to devote to your own primary issue—or favorite TV programs. One thing is clear: if we remain fixated on our own dime, we're likely to end up short of change.

If, on the other hand, we extend support to those struggling to lighten their own burdens, we just might pick up some unexpected allies for our own cause. I say "unexpected" because the gender binary and opposite-sex coupling still seem to many on the straight left as preordained by nature; they remain in thrall to the view that deviations from natural law are the disturbed doings of a marginal few, people to be avoided or discouraged. There's a chance, though, that if we're working side by side on a project of common interest, some purported truisms might come to seem less cast in stone than once thought.

Take prison reform, for example. Historically, as Regina Kunzel has amply demonstrated, Gay Liberation Front activists in 1970 staged several demonstrations in front of the Women's House of Detention (then located in the Village, subsequently torn down), calling up to the prisoners, "Power to the sisters!" and the prisoners calling back, "Power to the gay people!" Even after GLF became defunct, other gay groups maintained the connection; as Kunzel has written, "Political connections between lesbian and gay activists and prison inmates persisted as an important and under-recognized feature of the gay liberation movement of the 1970s. Many marches and demonstrations of the movement's early years chose jails and prisons as rallying sites."[11]

And not only in New York. Kunzel records demonstrations as well at Chicago's Cook County Jail and in Boston's Charles Street Jail—both in 1972. Gay activists also started a wide range of projects to draw attention to the prisoners' plight, including publicizing brutal prison conditions, lobbying legal counsel, and organizing pen pal outreach. And always, they referred to the prisoners as "brothers" and "sisters." None of it was easy, and none of it took place without discord and friction between the gay activists and the confined prisoners; some of the conflict reflected class and racial differences, and there was dissonance as well between prison's inbred insistence on rigid gender roles (you fuck or get fucked; you're a man or a woman) and the gay activists' androgynous ideal of gender deconstruction.

Yet as Kunzel makes clear, some of the interactions between prisoners and activists became—for both—transformational. Both of Boston's radical gay publications, *Fag Rag* and *Gay Community News,* ran free ads for prisoners and helped to run a prisoner book project with Redbook, the Cambridge-based radical bookstore. Mike Riegle, a member of the *Fag Rag* collective, who died of AIDS in 1992, conjoined conditions in and outside prison: "What's going on inside is only an exaggeration and a distortion of what's happening right out here, in what some of my prisoner friends call 'minimum custody.'" In language that resonates today, Riegle insisted on the connections between the "politics of crime" and "the general politics of social control, control of bodies, and even control of desires."[12]

Today, we still have openly gay leftists working strenuously on behalf of a variety of social justice issues; to give but one example, Alicia Garza and Patrisse Khan-Cullors, two of the three founders of Black Lives Matter, are queer women. And radical gay people *are* at work in other organizations pushing for substantive change. My point is that the *national* gay movement—reflecting, alas (or so it does currently seem), the priorities of the gay majority—itself remains in thrall to single-issue politics and to pledging allegiance to the institutions of an unjust social order.[13]

Nearly fifty years ago GLF activists lent their voices to progressive causes because they believed in them. Today, with "let us in" seemingly commanding far more allegiance among the gay majority than do calls to "change the system!" any argument for a *multi*-issue platform would need to stress its pragmatic rather than its moral urgency. And that's not an easy argument to make, even among those of us who are temperamental optimists. To persuade the gay majority that joining the struggle for a living wage or for prison reform would necessarily redound to its own advantage—would ultimately produce an end to all forms of legal discrimination, including against LGBTQ people—runs smack up against the reality of a still-entrenched homophobia that justifies its hostility not on our failure to engage in a broad-gauged politics of empathy but on the traditional conviction that same-gender love and lust are *abominations*.

"Nonsense!" one might say in response. "That view is no longer widely held; these days it's confined to far right, evangelical Christian circles." True—if you simply mean the term *abomination*. *Not* true if you take into account a different, more genteel vocabulary that speaks instead of the "sadness" of lives that aren't centered on family life and child-rearing. Being gay, in this commonly held view, is like being single—that is, second-rate, incomplete, not adult. Such lives are seen as stunted, abnormal, disfigured: "Something went wrong in the formative years which made these isolated, lonely people forever fearful of intimacy, narcissistically self-enclosed, constantly in pursuit of sex because they're in disastrous flight from love."

This version of homophobia is alive and well. It's the one entrenched in sophisticated straight circles that wouldn't dream of quoting Leviticus or of describing themselves as anything other than liberal—even radical. They openly disdain the primitive prejudices of evangelical Christians even as they secretly harbor a no less haughty form of intolerance against those who eschew a lifelong fidelity to family life, or who "cheat" on its confinements. The left-wingers among these sophisticates are themselves often critical of traditional institutions, and some would even challenge standard definitions of what constitutes a "healthy" libidinous life or a "significant" relationship." But they don't regard gender queers or sexual minorities as acceptable representatives of the good life—let alone as candidates for legal protection or allies in a political coalition.

The argument, in other words, that the gay majority and the organizations that represent it should broaden their social justice agendas can't pretend that an *inevitable* side benefit will be a gain in respect and acceptance from heterosexual left-wingers who currently hold us at arm's length—a result even less likely if we insist that they accept us for who we *really* are, rather than the synthetic version HRC is currently peddling to the public. Lending our weight to the eradication of such social iniquities as subsistence wage labor and police brutality may have to be its own reward. It's *possible* that a broadened gay agenda might soften our image and bolster our support among straight left-wingers, but the case for pessimism is in fact strong.

One emblematic example of the straight left's ongoing blindness to gay lives and indifference to our issues is captured in Heather Boushey's much-praised *Finding Time: The Economics of Work-Life Conflict.* Boushey outlines the necessity of forming a coalition to combat the inequities of American life, and lists as potential members those who advocate for workers, women, children, the elderly, the disabled—even people of faith!—and yet makes no mention of including the gay movement as a potential ally.[14]

The same is true of Naomi Klein's latest book, *No Is Not Enough*.[15] She, too, calls for a progressive coalition whose members will "pipe down about their individual grievances" and join forces in fighting against "global warming, racism, inequality, violations of Indigenous, migrant and women's rights," and she too omits gay rights groups from inclusion. She smartly argues that the "over-arching task" of the Left is not a "cage match" to rank our various issues, but to understand instead how they intersect and how we need to combine forces "to take on the pseudo-populist Right." Yet when these diverse constituencies met in June 2017 for a People's Summit to hash out a "broad-based 'People's Agenda,'" gay people were notable by their absence.

Some of the problem here is that on the whole our national organizations, and in particular the Human Rights Campaign, hasn't presented us as *interested* in any issues other than our own. If we present ourselves to the country—as HRC does—as patriotic centrists unconcerned, say, with stagnating workers' wages or the ongoing stigma of segregated schools, the Left will take us at our word and look elsewhere for allies in a left-wing coalition.

Still, the fault is certainly not ours alone. To some extent it's been *convenient* for the straight left to equate HRC with the whole of the gay movement, to ignore the fact that the majority of LGBTQ people are working-class and share in its privations, to tell itself that our purported "issues" revolve around where to find a good nanny or the difficulties of getting into the "right" kindergarten. If you quote to straight left-wingers the 2015 FBI statistic that nearly 19 percent of so-called "single bias" hate crimes were attributable to sexual orientation, they'll quote back at you the same report that 47 percent were attributable—still!—to race. Tell them that as a result primarily of bullying and violence, LGBTQ high school teenagers have far higher rates of depression and suicide than do their heterosexual peers, and they'll tell you that a larger percentage of black teenagers in New York City are attending—as a result of neighborhood segregation—inferior, highly segregated schools than was true forty years ago. Straight *black* leftists, unlike their white counterparts, don't need to be told that in 2017—fifty years after the landmark Supreme Court decision *Loving v. Virginia*—the well-regarded Ipsos poll found 35 percent of white Americans agreeing with the statement that "marriage should only be allowed between people of the same race"; the same poll reports nearly 40 percent agreeing that "white people are currently under attack in this country" and that "America must protect and preserve its White European heritage."[16]

I hasten to add that traditional homophobia ("Gays are sick") is unquestionably less embedded—at the least, less consciously embraced—on the Left than on the Right, where if anything it's been burgeoning of late (currently more than 150 pieces of anti-gay legislation are pending in twenty-nine state legislatures). Yet even if gay or feminist radicals of the new generation could somehow capture their own national movements, it isn't at all clear that the straight left would promptly elevate issues relating to sex and gender to the top of its agenda. Many straight leftists would likely argue that their plates are already full, and with issues that they consider far more important than whether it's advisable to delay trans surgery beyond the teen years or whether gay history should be added to the high school curriculum. That stuff is trivial, they'd likely say, when stacked up against the fact that most Americans still haven't recovered from the economic meltdown of 2008—the worst economic crisis since the Great Depression. The wealthy, on the other hand, are doing just fine—no, better than fine (the top 1 percent, according to the economist Emmanuel Saez, have won 91 percent of the nation's growth in income since 2009).

The statistics *are* appalling. The combined wealth of the country's four hundred richest Americans is greater than the bottom 61 percent of the population—in fact 42 percent of U.S. workers make less than $15 per hour (by global standards, of course, America's poor are wealthier than most of the world). Some 43 million people in the United States—13.5 percent of the population—are living in poverty, which is officially defined as having an annual income of roughly $24,000 for a family of four. Some economists argue that the official measure in fact underestimates the number of Americans who fall below the poverty line by failing to include such items as medical and work-related expenses. It's often forgotten, too, that a child growing up in poverty has a greatly reduced chance of getting a good education, a healthy diet, decent housing, a secure job, or the chance to save money for emergencies and retirement. Nor is the much-touted mobility of the American way a reality: we rank among the lowest among wealthy nations in the opportunities we offer for upward mobility.[17]

It gets worse: Oxfam reported in 2017 that just eight men, six of them Americans, now own the same amount of wealth as the poorer half of the world's population—meaning more than 3.6 billion people. Not the least of the many issues embedded in these statistics is the *attitude* rampant both at the top and the bottom: those at the top believe their success is due to their own talent and hard work; and many at the bottom still believe—contrary to all evidence—that they too might get rich if they worked harder or were smarter.[18]

This core bootstraps narrative of individualistic self-reliance has held firm throughout U.S. history, and it encourages the view that inequality essentially results from variations in skill and effort—with the inescapable corollary (so saith the Bible) that "the poor shall always be with you." It's enough to make one weep: those struggling to make ends meet not only continue to suffer—but continue to blame themselves for their plight. The average worker, paid minimal wages and denied payment for overtime, health care benefits, and paid sick leave, is rarely heard to complain that the CEO, who doesn't seem to be working any harder than they are, is earning $15 million (and up). Yet passivity prevails—and unionization continues to decline.

It wasn't always this way. In *The Age of Acquiescence*, Steve Fraser has refreshed our memory: resigned compliance has *not* always been the characteristic response of the American working class to wretched conditions. Fraser reminds us that throughout the late nineteenth and early twentieth centuries, working-class resistance was dynamic, prolonged, passionate, often physical—and aimed in the right direction (not, that is, at electing people like Trump). The social upheaval that accompanied industrialization was continuous and unrelenting, sabotage and arson were common, and violent skirmishes marked the culminating 1877 strike of railway workers—the "Great Uprising."

That particular insurrection failed, but the profound challenge it represented to capitalist exploitation resurfaced time and again for decades thereafter. Strikes were called, factories occupied, state militias brought in, and occasional pitched battles fought. The federal government proved a compliant handmaiden in protecting employer—not worker—rights, and the judiciary further obliged the corporate titans with injunctions and harsh sentences—including executions. After the Russian Revolution spread fear of contagion among the wealthy, the Woodrow Wilson administration calmed their nerves with a full-scale repression that included the abrupt deportation of Emma Goldman and her comrades (to Russia, of course). The slaughter of World War I put another large dent in the ranks of potential radicals.[19]

In the 1930s, FDR's New Deal reforms created a series of federal programs that helped to "civilize" capitalism; thanks to Social Security, paid vacations, and medical insurance, working-class resentment dissipated. Then, following World War II, the American economy boomed and unionized white workers prospered. But the interlude was brief; by the early seventies, a variety of factors, including the war in Vietnam and competition from a revitalized Europe and Japan, forced American companies to downsize, and capital fled overseas to take advantage of cheap labor and minimal regulation. The manufacturing economy faltered, membership in organized labor declined, free trade agreements proliferated, and the world of hedge funds and international finance flourished—abetted by President Reagan's appointment of antilabor members to the National Labor Relations Board and conservative judges to the bench. The average citizen, however, did not flourish: according to nearly every measure of general welfare (like home ownership and public health) the United States began a rapid slide in comparison with other developed nations.

By 2004, among thirty-one countries in the Organisation for Economic Cooperation and Development, the United States ranked twenty-fifth in the overall security of its citizens. As Stephanie Coontz has suggested, a vicious cycle was now set in motion: forced to pay more for expenses like transportation and medical care, lower-income workers came to resent taxes even when levied for services they needed, such as preschool and child care. Thus when President Obama called in his 2013 State of the Union address for universal pre-K and followed up with a proposal to fund a federal program for all four-year-olds from low- and moderate-income families with an increased tax on tobacco, the lack of grassroots support for such an increase allowed an unsympathetic Congress to bury the proposal.[20]

It's important to remember that the inequality gap wasn't always as large as it is currently. In their 2016 study, *Unequal Gains,* Peter Lindert and Jeffrey Williamson analyze a wide range of data from the pre-1870 period and conclude that during the colonial era the United States *was* a land of opportunity and "the best poor man's country in the world" (unless you were black, of course). Average income levels were higher than elsewhere, and as a result so was the general standard of living. As late as the mid-twentieth century, tax rates on the rich went at one point as high as 90 percent (and inheritance taxes reached 80 percent). All that has changed. John Maynard Keynes purportedly taught us long ago that the failure to regulate wealth is an obvious recipe for producing inequality, and since the 1970s an unregulated financial sector has steadily widened the gap between rich and poor.[21]

In the 1980s the trend accelerated, the result of interrelated factors that included technology, globalization, governmental policies favoring the rich, and a decline in the skill set of the average worker. Today only half of Americans in their thirties earn more than their parents did at that age—though the real economy has more than doubled in size since 1980. The weakening of labor unions and the rise of corporate *political* power (exemplified by President Trump's cabinet of billionaires) has produced the double whammy of stagnating wages and heightened wealth for the already rich. The share of total income that goes to the bottom half of the population has shrunk from 20 percent in 1980 to 12.5 percent in 2014. Concurrently, seven out of every ten dollars goes to the top tenth of the income scale, and the earnings of the top 1 percent have doubled since 1980. Put in dollars and cents, by 2014, the average income of half of American adults was around $16,000, while members of the top 1 percent brought home on average $1,304,800—or 81 times as much. Those in the lower 50 percent have been consoling themselves not by angry protest but by (when they can afford it) mounting consumerism. Bigger TVs have replaced bigger unions, but a gnawing discontent, an impotent feeling of emptiness, remains.[22]

None of this comes as news. We've known about the widening inequality gap for some time, and known, too, that in our so-called democracy the political system has been increasingly driven by money for money; the majority no longer rules. We're well aware, or should be, that the tax code is so full of loopholes that the rich line their pockets—and avoid taxes—with ease (the wealthiest four hundred American taxpayers, each with annual income over $100 million, have of late been paying a federal tax rate—thanks to deductions that include such items as the cost of buying a private plane—of 16 to 22 percent). They and their representatives in Congress apparently couldn't care less that for the average American, median wages have stalled, that full-time work—*without* benefits—is ever harder to find, and that more than half a million children in our country suffer from lead poisoning.[23]

To compound the plight of the average American, the New Deal–Great Society safety net has over the past twenty years become increasingly shredded. In 1996, 68 percent of families with children living in poverty received welfare; in 2016 only 23 percent did—though in that same time span the number of U.S. families living in *extreme* poverty (the global metric for which is households with incomes of less than $2 per person per day) increased 35 percent and included roughly three million American children. In September 2017 the U.S. Department of Agriculture released its annual report on hunger and "food insecurity" in the United States. Its conclusions are beyond shocking. The report classifies 41 million Americans as "food insecure," a figure that includes 13 million children who go to bed at night hungry—this at a time when the stock market has soared to unprecedented heights and the net worth of each of the four hundred wealthiest Americans rose by roughly $2.5 million.[24]

Can't they fall back on welfare? No, not easily. President Bill Clinton ended welfare as we knew it when he championed and signed the Personal Responsibility Act in 1996, tying welfare to work. Though the bill was shorn of some of the worst measures the Republicans had argued for—like taking children away from unwed teen mothers and putting them in orphanages—its administration was shifted to the states, with little federal oversight. Not surprisingly, the states have used the block grants as a kind of all-purpose slush fund; the amount actually going to desperately needy families fell from 68 percent in 1996 to 23 percent in 2014. The 1996 act *did* succeed in pushing poor families with children off the welfare rolls—not into decent paying jobs, but into living on two dollars a day.[25]

An increasing number of available jobs these days are in the service sector—predominantly in health care, fast food, and retail sales—and they're often defined by no benefits, low wages (the median annual wage of a health aide is $21,850), and irregular hours. It's not surprising that nearly half of working-age families have literally zero retirement savings and that for many of those who do, the median retirement account is between $15,000 and $20,000. The basic goods and services that many Americans before 1980 were likely to cite as defining a "good" life are today beyond the reach of the average worker. The floor has fallen away.

And especially for people of color. The Great Cities Institute at the University of Illinois at Chicago issued a report in 2016 that put their plight into figures: In Los Angeles and New York City roughly 30 percent of twenty-to-twenty-four-year-old black men were out of work and out of school in 2014; in Chicago the figure was 50 percent. The rate for Hispanic men in the same age group was 20 percent—and for white men 10 percent. The situation has become critical for black Americans. According to a 2016 report from the Economic Policy Institute, black Americans today earn less relative to their white counterparts than they did in 1979. Average hourly wages for black men went from being 22.2 percent lower than those of white males to being 31 percent lower by 2015, while the wage gap for black women went from 6 percent in 1979 to 19 percent in 2015.[26]

Yet as Nicholas Kristof has written in the *New York Times,* fully "half of white Americans continue to believe that discrimination against whites is as big a problem as discrimination against blacks." Which runs directly counter to the massive amount of research showing that blacks are more likely than whites (as Kristof puts it) "to receive longer sentences, to be discriminated against in housing, to be denied job interviews, to be rejected by doctors' offices, to suffer bias in almost every measurable sector of daily life"—and, in addition, to being routinely assigned to underfunded, third-rate schools and subjected to the systemic racism of our criminal justice system. Yet House Speaker Paul Ryan, as recently as 2016, has dared to argue that aid to the poor is ultimately counterproductive because it undermines the incentive to work, and his Republican minions still threaten to roll back the remaining lifelines of Medicaid and the Affordable Care Act. Since Ryan and his cohorts don't seem notably stupid, the inescapable conclusion is that they're morally obtuse—and perhaps criminally callous.[27]

Put in a global context, American workers are still better off than those in most of the world (though certainly not those in Europe and Scandinavia), where roughly 10 percent of the planet's population—a decline over recent decades—lives in extreme poverty. In his book *The Great Leveler* (2017) Walter Scheidel goes so far as to suggest that "only all-out thermonuclear war might fundamentally reset the existing distribution of resources."[28] Or—compressing the disaster scenario into a single word—violence. Americans are certainly prone to it, though they generally vent against fellow sufferers—or the terrorists they're told are everywhere threatening to destroy them. Short of a domestic conflagration—neither feasible, desirable, or likely (given the penchant of average Americans to blame *themselves* for their misfortunes)—we somehow need to find the will to stand up to such abominations, as we did a hundred years ago during the first Gilded Age. A countervailing power has to be brought to bear on the grotesque disparities that currently disfigure our society, threatening to transform it permanently into an oligarchy (if it hasn't done so already).

The countervailing force of organized labor at certain periods in our history did much to curtail—albeit mostly for white men—some of the grosser abuses of the American Way. And there are those who feel it might again, though even the optimists seem aware of the poor odds. The good blue-collar jobs that fueled much of post–World War II prosperity have nearly disappeared. The newer, service jobs make up what one labor expert, Tamara Draut, has called our current "bargain-basement economy." Unlike the industrial economy that preceded it, the service economy is distinguished by the absence of protection for workers. Typically, they lack paid vacations, health and disability insurance, parental leave, child care support, pensions—and even regular working hours. *In*stability is the new economy's most notable feature.

In the past, strong unions provided for a far better working environment than is currently the case. In the mid-1950s one-third of all American workers belonged to a union; by 2015 that number had dwindled to a mere 11 percent. The federal government made a major contribution to this decline with passage of the Taft-Hartley Act in 1947, which enabled the states to pass so-called right-to-work laws that banned the closed shop and thereby weakened a union's ability to speak in a strong collective voice. Simultaneously the business community became increasingly emboldened in lobbying Congress for free trade agreements, pushing for deregulation and automation, outsourcing more and more jobs to low-wage countries overseas, and permanently banning workers who went on strike. Meanwhile, the growing diversity within the workforce has brought with it rising racial tensions, further weakening labor's ability to respond to mounting corporate aggression. The gradual decline in union membership has turned into a catastrophic free fall—and a forty-year stagnation in wages.

Today labor organizers and labor historians alike are sharply divided about how—and even whether—to restore union power to its former strength. To a layman like me, it seems obvious that the historical conditions that once made mass unionization and militancy possible cannot be recovered, that the era of lifelong employment in a single industry, with the industry itself rooted in one spot geographically, is gone forever. The hope is that new coalitions will emerge with enough bargaining power to apply the needed pressure for change—with the central components possibly being the young radicals who formed Occupy Wall Street and later fueled Bernie Sanders's presidential campaign, or—much less likely—possibly the formation and combination of workers' cooperatives such as exist in parts of Europe.

The current debate about the continuing relevance of trade unionism has divided expert opinion. Jane McAlevey is among the more prominent labor leaders who believe that unions, and the latent power of collective bargaining, retain their vital potential. McAlevey spent five years as executive director of Local 1107 of the Service Employees International Union (SEIU), one of the country's largest and most powerful unions, and saw firsthand that union-busting relies heavily on pitting ethnic and racial divisions within the labor force against one another. She claims to have learned as well that traditional hands-on, bottom-up—and aggressive—organizing produces better results than faceless new techniques like tweets and polls. McAlevey has on her side of the argument the fact that in a few economically advanced countries, union membership still remains over 50 percent—though unlike the United States, such countries allow their unions to administer unemployment benefits, thereby helping to build and solidify constituencies.[29]

Andy Stern, former president of the 2.2 million–member SEIU, has a very different view. His wide-ranging assessment of labor's future rests on the irreducible fact that millions of well-paid, full-time jobs have disappeared; only 8 percent of the country's jobs are currently in manufacturing (compared to 24 percent in 1960)—and thanks to the accelerating pace of automation, they aren't coming back. That alone, Stern argues, makes any attempt to rebuild the bargaining power of unions a fool's errand. Though it's been suggested that labor might try to augment its power by focusing on organizing some of the larger new formations of the postindustrial economy (such as universities and hospitals), Stern dismisses that suggestion, too, as a forlorn hope.[30]

He has a different solution in mind for meliorating economic inequality: a guaranteed, fixed basic income for every adult citizen between the ages of eighteen and sixty-four. As someone who's long advocated a guaranteed annual income, though I lack Stern's experience and knowledge, I found his argument compelling (but I think his suggested $12,000 a year is inadequate—$25,000 would be more like it). The experts remain divided about the likely course of automation in the coming years, yet few seem to doubt that there'll be a diminished need for human labor. If the federal government could finally undertake a long-overdue revamping of our antiquated infrastructure, a short-term boost in employment would surely follow—though given the size of the national debt and the ever-voracious maw of "national defense," nobody's holding their breath. Shorter work weeks coupled with significant increases in hourly wages could also temporarily stem the tide—but not even that will happen so long as senators like Mitch McConnell continue to man the rowboats.

In the face of unstoppable automation and the accelerated disappearance of jobs, why *not* a guaranteed annual income? It would put a floor to the massive misery that looms ahead and would give people something they haven't had in a long time (or perhaps ever): enough leisure to enjoy their lives, to develop their interests and talents, to spend time with their loved ones. People could—imagine!—actually *choose* how they want to spend the bulk of their time.

The idea of a guaranteed income isn't, as Stern points out, a new one. Tom Paine proposed it (in *Agrarian Justice*) back in 1795.

Bertrand Russell got on board in his 1918 book *Roads to Freedom*. The United Nations' 1948 Universal Declaration of Human Rights insists that "everyone has the right to a standard of living adequate for the health and well-being of himself and of his family." Other notables have also championed the idea, including John Kenneth Galbraith, Martin Luther King Jr., *and* the conservative economists F. A. Hayek and Milton Friedman. And in 1969—though this is hard to believe in today's mean-spirited climate—a presidential commission (the president being Nixon, no less) unanimously recommended the adoption of a guaranteed income—with *no* work requirements. The House of Representatives actually passed such a bill, but it died in the Senate.

Then there's Alaska's "Permanent Fund." Ever hear of it? I hadn't either, until I read Stern's book. Each Alaskan gets an annual dividend (depending on the price of oil) that has worked out over the years to about $2,000 per person. Stern tells us that, unsurprisingly, it's "enormously popular." The Cherokee Indians in North Carolina have done still better; thanks to profits from their casino, each of their 8,000 members receives about $6,000 a person yearly. The results have been entirely positive: high school graduation rates have gone up, mental health and substance abuse have gone down. The problem with poverty, it turns out, is pretty simple: a lack of income.

The standard response to this good news—usually delivered in a tone of maximum outrage—is that giving people money will inevitably "sap their initiative!" To which I'd reply, Nothing saps initiative—or produces zombie-like depression and alienation—more than the tedious, repetitive, noncreative work that many Americans are forced to perform—when they can get it—for eight hours a day in order to survive. The guaranteed income gives the individual the power to say No!—or, conversely, the power to take control of some of life's basic decisions.[31]

By way of example, Stern shows us the results of a basic income experiment conducted during 2008–9 in an impoverished region of Namibia. There was, according to Stern, an *increase* in entrepreneurship during the period ("average income grew 39 percent beyond the basic income"), with many recipients starting their own small businesses—baking bread, making bricks, and sewing dresses. Other positive results included a decrease in the dependency of women on men, a steep (40 percent) decline in school dropout rates, and a significant drop in household debt. What was that you said about lack of initiative? It's *welfare,* not a guaranteed income, that discourages people from working—for the simple reason that under it your benefits go down if your income goes up.

Should the guaranteed annual income somehow come to pass, and with it a more equitable society, the Andy Sterns don't have much to tell us about what a more leisured new world might (or ideally should) look like. Much like Marx before them, they're better at analyzing what's currently wrong and how we could set it to rights than in describing in any detail the utopia that might ultimately follow. Yes, Stern does parenthetically mention that we'll have more leisure time to explore our interests, talents, and relationships, but he seems to assume that the "we" who'll be doing the exploring will be much like the "we" we know today. If so, isn't the likelihood great that we'll somehow manage to reproduce the mess we're desperately trying to get out of? Put another way, if humanity continues to consist of (to oversimplify) grubby predators and benumbed victims, we're doomed to reproduce the same institutions and promote the same values that have carried us this far down the road to oblivion.

And that raises the question of whether the human product we see around us is unfit to inhabit any genuinely new world that might arise. If such is the case, that means we have to start talking—as the Andy Sterns are not—about the need for innovative forms of education and parenting that *might* help bring into existence a generation capable of using its newfound leisure to displace currently hegemonic values of rapacity and self-absorption. Further, we might crawl out from the rigid social and economic roles most of us are trained to inhabit and develop a less cramped, more exploratory sense of our potential—and that of others.

But I'm getting ahead of myself. Newfound leisure can come into being only if we succeed in creating a more equitable distribution of wealth and of the increase in free time that would follow. And that in turn hinges on a powerful left-wing movement that succeeds in reallocating the planet's resources. Sarah Leonard and Bhaskar Sunkara, in a coda to their edited anthology *The Future We Want: Radical Ideas for the New Century*, point to the "new signs of life" that have been emerging on the Left, and they locate its core in the awareness "that elites use their wealth and power to the detriment of the vast majority of people"—an insight that "has introduced a level of class analysis into the national public debate unseen in eight years."[32]

To combat this concentration of wealth and power, Leonard and Sunkara envision a coalition that would include "outgrowths of new protest movements, like Occupy Wall Street and Black Lives Matter, and more recent labor insurgencies." But—a now familiar pattern—they make no mention at all either of the feminist or LGBTQ movements as potential components of this new coalition; the unspoken assumption is that these groups don't share the wish to fight against concentrated power, that their agendas are dominated instead with bourgeois preoccupations like "gender fluidity" and polyamorous sex. (The charge directly echoes the Old Left's indictment of the 1960s counterculture.) But Leonard and Sunkara are, disturbingly, conflating the mainstream national gay movement with the quite different agenda of newly emergent radical grassroots LGBTQ groups.

The Future We Want does include one essay, Kate Redburn's (discussed earlier), that deals cogently, though incompletely, with the current gay movement. Like the anthology's other contributors, Redburn emphasizes the paramount importance of economic issues, and she accurately sees the mainstream gay agenda as driven by a "handful of organizations" that focus on "gay rights over collective social justice." She points out further that recently only 4 percent of foundation money given for LGBTQ issues has gone "to fighting violence and transphobia and only 2 percent toward economic issues"—in comparison to the 40 percent that goes to civil rights issues. I share Redburn's indignation "that this leaves trans people and queer youth twice vulnerable: they lack access to the resources of the wealthy, and they are marginalized for being queer."[33]

But I don't share her either-or conclusion that "their status cannot be improved with rights alone, but only through a radical redistribution of wealth and power." No, civil rights protections—which can be defined to include a radical renovation of the criminal justice system, policing, and immigration policy—can do something, if not everything, to ease the endemic pain of those minority communities, especially since the "radical redistribution of wealth and power" isn't exactly on the immediate horizon and the mainstream gay Human Rights Campaign seems uninterested in trying to engage the problem.

Like Redburn, I lament the mainstream gay movement's emphasis on "social inclusion," on "having access to the same sources of power as comparably situated straight people"— rather than on "challenging the distribution of power that creates inequity in the first instance." Yet when she calls for the mainstream gay movement's "marriage machine" to redirect its energy "at broader policies affecting economic inequality," I think she must know that the likelihood is negligible. And that's what makes her charge to queer and trans people "to drive the [mainstream gay] movement toward connecting with ongoing struggles to raise the minimum wage, build affordable housing, promote reproductive justice, and end mass incarceration" sound unrealistic—and out of touch. Queer and trans people *don't* drive the mainstream movement's agenda, and it's sheer fantasy to suggest that they could *if only they made the effort.*

Besides—and importantly—the straight left hasn't exactly put out the welcome mat or extended a helping hand (well, a pinkie maybe) to queer and trans people. In any case, whatever hope there is of "driving" the mainstream gay movement to include economic issues lies with the emergent radical gay local organizations—of which Redburn *is* aware—though the hope is slim, given the middle-class mind-set of the gay majority, which seems in no hurry to pressure its national organizations to shift emphasis from acceptance of income inequality to a pointed campaign to work against it.

Even when aware of the gay left's existence, which is rare, the straight left's disinterest in it (in my opinion, a polite cover for contempt) is a reflection both of homegrown homophobia and of a worldwide backlash against the centrist gains of the gay mainstream in recent decades. A certain amount of backlash always follows a period of substantive change. Yet the retrenchment of the past few years in regard to gay rights seems deeper than most. The Pew Research Center has isolated what it calls "the global divide on homosexuality." On one side are Western Europe and the United States, on the other most of Africa, the Middle East, and the post-communist world; the former has seen a strong attempt to roll back gay rights, the latter a determined effort to prevent them from ever gaining root.[34]

In Europe massive protests have been mounted against same-sex marriage; in Brazil the legislature has passed a series of antigay bills, and the country has seen a wave of gay killings (three thousand since the mid-eighties). One of the stronger backlashes has been in the United States: between 1998 and 2012, some thirty states enacted constitutional bans on same-sex marriage, and since the Supreme Court decision in 2013 striking down the Defense of Marriage Act (DOMA), an additional 254 antigay bills have been introduced, most of them under cover of "protecting religious freedom," some of them—the so-called "bathroom bills"—requiring that trans people must use public bathrooms appropriate to the gender assigned them on their birth certificates.

In Africa, the Middle East, and the post-communist countries, there has been outright repression and murder. Seventy-two countries officially label homosexuality a crime, and in three—Iran, Saudi Arabia, and Yemen—conviction brings the death penalty; in five others—Afghanistan, Mauritania, Pakistan, Qatar, and the United Arab Emirates—Shariah law also demands death for homosexuality but the sentence hasn't, as yet, been put into practice. In 2009 Uganda passed legislation calling for the death penalty for those committing "the offence of homosexuality" (later "lightened" to life imprisonment).

Russia's "gay propaganda law" is written broadly enough to include prohibition of Pride parades, same-sex displays of affection, gay publications and films, and even the rainbow flag. In Chechnya, the pro-Kremlin leader Ramzan A. Kadyrov has arrested, tortured, and in at least three cases, killed gay men; some have died at the hands of their own relatives in "honor killings." In South Korea, powerful Christian groups have launched an intense campaign against homosexuality, and all candidates in the recent presidential campaign spouted a primitive brand of homophobia.

These horrific incidents are scarcely known in the United States, thanks largely to an American provincialism that assumes the only actions and attitudes that matter are our own. And this is true of gay as well as straight Americans, though less true of gays on the left. The international community, fortunately, *has* begun to take up the issue of antigay violence—or at least begun passing resolutions. The United Nations Human Rights Commission enacted a resolution in 2011 that called for the decriminalization of homosexuality, and in May 2016 the UN Security Council condemned violence against LGBT people—the first time that body had ever mentioned homosexuality. Still, LGBTQ people in general, and trans people in particular, remain subject to random verbal abuse and physical attack. As I write this (in February 2018), President Trump is poised to sign a "religious liberty" executive order granting individuals and groups exemption on religious grounds from a whole array of federal laws, including those referencing same-sex marriage, trans identity, and premarital sex. The War on Sex is proceeding with a vengeance.[35]

If the straight left is concerned about any of this, their lamentations haven't reached my ears. I've read pretty widely in the recent literature and the anguished focus of attention—even among young leftists (supposedly more sympathetic than their elders to gay and feminist concerns)—is almost exclusively economic; conversely, the gay left's interest in economics ranges from anemic to nonexistent. Take for example Jonathan Matthew Smucker's recent *Hegemony How-To*, a comprehensive and valuable "roadmap for radicals" (its subtitle). In his 280-page book, Smucker never mentions bisexuality, and slips in "gay" parenthetically a grand total of three times (I may have missed one or two), "feminism" twice, and "transgender" once—and *mentions* is the accurate word. Nothing remotely resembling an analysis of those movements is attempted; by implication, the message gets conveyed that they're irrelevant as potential contributors to the *serious* "left hegemonic project" Smucker feels will likely become a realistic possibility in the decades ahead. He lyrically describes that future as one in which "there is more compassion and social justice," yet apparently isn't aware or doesn't agree that challenges to traditional notions of gender and sexuality are—or should be—critical elements in a unified social justice movement.[36]

Smucker does well to warn "underdog groups ... to vigilantly resist the tendency of insularity and self-enclosure" (the heart of my own complaint against the Human Rights Campaign), yet when characterizing "the radical project" of "collective human liberation," he makes no reference at all to GLF's expansive past efforts along those lines nor to the galaxy of emancipatory projects currently being put forward by radical local gay groups—who reject (to Smucker's deafening lack of applause) insular, single-issue politics. Similarly, when Smucker quotes Paulo Freire's now-famous (and wise) advice that we continuously foreground the question "What can we do now in order to be able to do tomorrow what we are unable to do today?" he never once references the cautionary example of GLF—which went asunder in the early seventies not simply due to cooptation by liberal reformers, but because of the same visionary "prefigurative" politics that later brought down Occupy Wall Street (which he *does* discuss at length).

Smucker recounts in *Hegemony How-To* his own years of involvement in radical organizing, yet despite his varied activities with a wide array of groups, he seems never to have run across any LGBTQ people. He does mention, curiously, that for a time he did PR for the Chelsea Manning Support Network, yet he does not describe his time at the network, leaving us to wonder, perhaps unfairly, if he thought the people involved were too trivial to linger over.

Smucker rightly places at the center of his message a call for uniting "hitherto fragmentary political actors"—to my mind essential in the effort to build a "resistance" of real strength. As possible components for such a coalition, he lists all the likely candidates—labor unions, community groups, religious congregations, Black Lives Matter, immigrant Dreamers, students—and *does* mention (in passing) "movements for gender justice and sexual liberation." Yet the only gay movement he actually names—and praises—is, weirdly, the "impressive campaign that mobilized the support of millions" on behalf of gay marriage. Say what? Is Smucker nominating for inclusion in his *radical* coalition the utterly mainstream marriage campaign that gay radicals strenuously protested?

What's going on here? In singling out the marriage campaign as the one gay accomplishment worthy of notice, Smucker is implicitly aligning himself with a centrist, assimilationist politics he ordinarily deplores. Is Smucker even aware that a gay left exists, that it shares much of his agenda and is ripe for inclusion in a left-wing coalition of "fragmentary political actors"? If so, you'd never know it. Never once does he even mention such radical activist gay groups, past and present, as Queer Nation, FIERCE, Women's Action Coalition, Queers for Economic Justice, Sex Panic!, the Combahee River Collective, and the Esperanza Peace and Justice Center. I don't know whether to ascribe his failure to discuss such groups as a function of his ignorance or his disapproval.

Either way, his treatment of the LGBTQ left wing is emblematic of the straight left's obliviousness—which I read as disdain—toward potential gay allies. It's difficult not to draw two unpleasant, intertwined conclusions. Like almost all of the articulate straight left, Smucker applauds the campaign for gay marriage in order to signal what he mistakenly believes is a sign of enlightened tolerance—even while simultaneously implying, intentionally or not, that the marriage issue is, after all, the only sort of mainstream preoccupation that can be hoped for from dippy, shallow queers. Let them and their feminist friends play in the infantile sandbox of sex and gender while we serious-minded revolutionaries address the foundational struggles against capitalism and imperialism.

Peter Frase's *Four Futures,* a much-admired book of impressive intelligence and scope, provides yet another example of how the straight left ignores or downplays any coalition role for the LGBTQ community. Frase's central argument is that accelerated automation, in combination with the scarcity of resources that will result from climate change, spells the end of capitalism as we know it. He believes that "no force is on hand that could be expected to reverse the three downward trends in economic growth, social equality and financial stability and end their mutual reinforcement." Frase then proceeds to outline four possible scenarios of what a post-capitalist world might look like, inviting fellow leftists to speculate on their comparative merits.[37]

It doesn't seem to have occurred to him that feminists and gay people should be invited to join the argument—let alone that they might have something of interest to contribute. Those movements go entirely unremarked in his book, and this obliteration typifies the attitude of most straight left-wing intellectuals: they either ignore us entirely or offhandedly mention that, yes, we do exist and, yes, we have a right to—but our concerns are irrelevant to Serious Thinkers on the Left. Apparently Frase is—yet again, like the straight left in general—conflating the centrist views of the Human Rights Campaign—which admittedly *does* represent the views of most gay people (or at least the minority that involves itself to any degree with politics)—with the entirety of the gay movement. Yet it's not difficult to see how the input of *left-wing* LGBTQ people might well be of value during the struggle to create a worthwhile post-capitalist world.

Convinced that capitalism's days are numbered (a hypothesis, not a proven fact), Frase—in one particularly incisive section—analyzes how "work" as we currently experience it might look in the future. For too many people today, work is something we do to survive—and given the deadly monotony of most jobs and the torpor it induces, "survival" has little to do with joy or satisfaction (especially since, as Frase perceptively adds, "men don't want to actually *be* useful, they merely want to 'feel' useful"). In a better future, he suggests, we'd participate in particular activities "because we found them inherently fulfilling, not because we needed a wage or owed our monthly hours to the cooperative." That ideal situation, Frase notes, *does* currently characterize the lives of a privileged few: they genuinely *choose* to work at what they do, not simply to put food on the table. For many of the rest of us, the experience of something resembling "happiness" comes not from work, but from the moment we're able to "retire" from it.

Frase is very much drawn to the views of the French socialist André Gorz, who dismissed the tired left-wing debate between "reform and revolution"—that is, whether it's possible to use traditional institutions like labor unions or the ballot box to overturn capitalism or whether a violent seizure of power is necessary. He quotes with approval the alternative Gorz suggested in his influential 1967 book, *Strategy for Labor:* "the possibility of 'revolutionary reforms,' that is to say, those that advance us 'toward a radical transformation of society'"—in contrast to what Gorz calls "reformist reforms" (for example, assimilation—the greater inclusion of more people into preexisting institutions). Gorz defines "revolutionary reforms" as those "determined not in terms of what can be, but what should be." Among such reforms, Gorz lists the guaranteed annual income.[38]

What Gorz does not list are the lifestyle changes that in the 1960s were known as the counterculture, just as Frase does not list, in quoting and recommending Gorz, the cultural challenges to traditional notions of gender and sexuality currently taking place all around *him.* Nor do his fellow (male) leftists. To do so would necessarily risk a confrontation with normative male values—which are cultural, not genetic—at the heart, it can be argued, of what currently troubles the world.

It's precisely those values of male dominance and aggression that the radical wings of the feminist and gay movements have challenged, and that the male-dominated Left continues to ignore them suggests a dimly perceived awareness that to confront them head-on with the seriousness they deserve is to imperil the foundations, personal and political, on which their own sense of entitlement rests. Capitalism is not the sole enemy (though it's real enough), nor is economic restructuring the sole solution. Heteronormative culture, with its emphasis on consumerism and its limited challenge to traditional maleness, has not simply emptied our pockets but also rotted our hearts and minds.

These are large assertions, and it might be best to approach them obliquely. I'll start with a twenty-year-old book, *Unheroic Conduct*, that I've never seen cited by the straight male Left—and only rarely, to be fair, by the gay left, either. Its author is Daniel Boyarin, a leading Talmudic scholar, and his main argument centers on Ashkenazic Jewish culture and how its view of masculinity was the polar opposite of the model that held sway under the Roman Empire. The ideal Roman man was a warrior—aggressively arrogant, violent, ruthless, and dominant. He saw the world as a testing ground for his own prowess, and the rest of humanity as servile accessories to his unimpeded rule.[39]

The Ashkenazic Jew, in contrast, was admired by his coreligionists for traits diametrically opposite: for gentleness and inwardness, for a studious abstention from worldly distractions. About all he shared with the pugilistic Roman was the conviction that women were created to serve him and were not to share in his exclusive access to power and authority. In the context of our own culture, the Ashkenazic male would likely be derided as a "sissy," though in his own day he was a revered model of ideal masculinity.

Boyarin urges us to reclaim that view of gentle manliness, arguing, perhaps extravagantly, that the "critical recovery of the past would make for the redemption of the future." Boyarin makes no effort to conceal his appreciation of the well-built male body—but a naturally healthy body, not the stereotypic muscularity of the gym-built superstud. He in fact specifically deplores the latter, warning that "the dimorphism of the gendered body ... participates in the general cultural standard of masculinity rather than resisting it," reinforcing the valorization of "topness" over receptivity that already disfigures our embedded norms. The dominant or dominant-looking male, it can be argued (persuasively, I think), is already excessively equated with normality—and *normal* gay males are being welcomed into the mainstream in ever-mounting numbers, even as the guards at the gates continue to bar admission to those who are behaviorally "queer."

But you cannot transform a culture by emulating its values. You cannot dispel the high esteem with which the macho male is held by becoming a hypermasculinized Navy Seal, nor heighten your regard for androgyny by studying army training manuals. "Is there a male masculinity for us to desire," Richard Rambuss asks in his essay "After Male Sex," "that isn't masculinist?" His answer (to the extent that he offers one) is curious: he confesses reluctance to reduce the "single-sexedness" of masculinist homoerotic sites like pornography or all-male sex clubs to "misogyny," arguing that the erotics of "virility" need not be "coextensive with a patriarchy that enjoins a political gendered inequality." And he pretty much leaves it at that. Well, as I've said, transformation isn't part of the mainstream gay agenda.[40]

In fact, some gay men—more, it would appear, in the generation now arriving than in the one exiting—consciously cultivate personality traits like empathy and altruism traditionally associated with "femaleness," and they score consistently higher on studies that attempt to measure such traits. They perceive discrimination against others more readily than do straight men; are more likely to have friends across lines of color, gender, religion, and politics; and, as one large-scale study concluded, volunteer 61 percent more time to nonprofit organizations than do their heterosexual counterparts.

In general, moreover, gay men put a higher premium on emotional expressiveness and sexual exploration than straight men do. They also work harder at both their friendships and their couple relationships to ensure mutuality and egalitarianism. The *New York Times* (no less) summarized a growing body of scholarly evidence suggesting that gay couples are "far more egalitarian than heterosexual ones" in sharing responsibility for both housework and finances, whereas in heterosexual relationships, women are still doing most of the domestic chores and as a result are living with a lot more anger than their male partners. When conflict arises, according to the *Times,* gay couples are less "belligerent and domineering" when arguing, and the partners make fewer verbal attacks on each other, are better at using humor and affection to defuse confrontation, and show much greater ability at "seeing the other person's point of view." In short, the *Times* editorialized, gay people "have a great deal to teach everyone else."[41]

Yes, precisely. That's the whole point—the one that continues to elude most straight male leftists. They apparently can't imagine that *we* might have anything of value to tell *them*— either about their personal lives or about their politics. And what continues in turn to elude most white *gay* men as well— yes, even as far back as the Gay Liberation Front—is how much our own awareness could be heightened by closer ties to women, people of color, and trans people.

None of those categories, including "gay male," should be taken as describing fixed identities. Singly and together, we span the horizon, our uniqueness as telling as the traits we share in common. Our states of being are neither fixedly predetermined nor airtight, and our fluid, contradictory natures themselves sit atop a barely buried hodgepodge of anarchic, not entirely controllable impulses. We're all "gender discordant," we're all sexual outlaws—that is, once we get around to listening more fully to ourselves (including our dreams and fantasies). Mostly, though, we keep the news secret, from ourselves and others. The invitation to expand and change is too scary.

The obstacles to forging a political alliance to combat the atrocities that mark our public life are large. I don't pretend to have the insight needed to distinguish them all. Besides, my "facts" may not be yours—and, as Nietzsche reminded us, there *aren't* any facts, only interpretations. My own sense, for what it's worth, is that lying deep in the unexplored recesses of the psyche lies a terrified fear (easily transformed into hate) of differentness, and that fear will likely surface when the prospect looms of connecting too closely with what is (or what we decide is) consequentially foreign.

Ideally, we would need the straight left (including feminism) and the gay left to combine forces. We would need straight male lefties to understand that the destruction of economic inequality—itself a goal nearly as inconceivable as it is desirable—will not alone make gladsome every hearth and home, that to complete the trinity and find congenial work and caring connection, a settled sense of safety and satisfaction, we must first endure what can be no less than a searing confrontation with the spectral myths of American benevolence.

As for the mainstream gay movement, we need it to open its heart and resources to first acknowledging and then helping to ameliorate the suffering of those queer people who refuse to inhabit an assigned gender, to those people of color who continue to suffer from a lack of jobs and massive incarceration for minor offenses (not to mention still being held back by inferior education, voting discrimination, residential segregation, and second-rate medical care), and to the sexual minorities who understand that kissing and cuddling can provide comfort, and sucking and fucking release, yet still don't exhaust the range of their expressive needs.

In regard to those needs, it hasn't been widely understood that the triumphalist narrative of homosexual emancipation largely leaves unmentioned the fact that when the Supreme Court in *Lawrence v. Texas* in 2003 decriminalized "sodomy," it did so *only* for consenting adults in private. Left unmentioned—and still criminalized—are those multitudes whose sexual lives do not match up with middle-class notions of morality, who do not (unlike the supporters of the Human Rights Campaign) regard matrimony, the child-rearing couple, monogamy, and the picket fence as the signposts not only of contented bliss but of mental health.

For both gay and straight minorities whose sexual habits fall outside prescribed parameters—including teenagers below the age of sixteen who make love together, polyamorists, sex workers, practitioners of S-M, public sex, and open marriages—the sex offender registry, not the welcome mat, shadows their doorstep. In other words, the status of a wide range of sexual behaviors that do not fit the approved license that *Lawrence v. Texas* handed out to "consenting adults in private" remains, in essence, unprotected—outside the law. And this is not theoretical. In some states the number of inmates incarcerated for "sexual offences" is as high as 30 percent.

Today "opposition to things as they are"—the "Resistance"—is widespread. Yet the parts do not cohere, and may never—not without a seismic effort to overcome our penchant for single-issue politics that caters solely to our own primary concerns. The amount of suffering in this country, when compared to its resources, is iniquitous. If we are ever to reduce it, we must combine with allies who we don't love but who share with us a common enemy—the country's oligarchic structure, its patriarchal authority, and its primitively fundamentalist moral values. Which means further that we must engage with our own dread and trepidation of the "other," and join forces for the common good. Will a sufficient number of outsiders prove gallant enough to run the gauntlet, to stay steadfastly in place when the dragon spits the full force of its fire in our direction? One can make a superficial guess and try predicting the unknowable, but the outcome will surprise us nonetheless. At least we hope it will.

Notes

PROLOGUE

1. Scott De Orio, "The Invention of Bad Gay Sex: Texas and the Creation of a Criminal Underclass of Gay People," *Journal of the History of Sexuality* 26, No. 1 (Jan. 2017).

2. As well, I'm grateful to Allen for letting me read a draft of his autobiography-in-progress; he expects to self-publish it in 2018.

3. Martin Duberman, *Stonewall* (Dutton, 1993), 173–75, 219–21.

ONE. STORMING THE CITADEL

1. Pam Mitchell, ed., *Pink Triangles: Radical Perspectives on Gay Liberation* (Alyson, 1980), 177; Alan Sinfield, *Gay and After* (Serpent's Tail, 1998), 20.

2. Published by Pomegranate Press; Canada's Pink Triangle Press subsequently reprinted the pamphlet in 1977.

3. Lisa Rapaport, "Millennial Hookup Culture May Not Be a Real Thing," *Reuters,* Aug. 2, 2016, https://www.reuters.com/article/us-health-millenials-sex/millennial-hookup-culture-may-not-be-a-real-thing-idUSKCN10D2IX; Lisa Wade, *American Hookup* (W.W. Norton, 2017); *New York Review of Books,* Aug. 18, 2016 (CDC; Ornstein).

4. Jillian Deri, *Love's Refraction* (University of Toronto Press, 2015), as quoted in Jean Roberta's review in *The Gay and Lesbian Review* (Jan.–Feb. 2016), 45.

5. Hodges and Hutter, *With Downcast Gays*, 11–12, 25–27.

6. The quotes in this and the following paragraph are from Thom Willenbecher, "Martin Duberman," *Esplanade* (June 17, 1977). Ten years later, and despite the AIDS epidemic, I was still expressing comparable sentiments in my diary: "The experts in nutrition acknowledge & encourage an 'instinctive' human craving for dietary variety. We need to transfer that insight to the area of sex. Hands will of course fly to the American face in instant horror—'Oh no! the *sexual* instinct is to mate with one partner, forever.' But 'instinct' cannot—or rather, should not—be invoked solely to confirm pre-existing values. Especially since no-one has successfully isolated and described our so-called 'instinctive' needs—even as everyone carelessly evokes them. *If* there are any human instincts at all, it will be difficult to defend the notion that they can be selectively divided—that is, an 'instinct' for variation in diet arrayed against an 'instinct' for consistency in sex."

7. David P. McWhirter and Andrew M. Mattison, *The Male Couple: How Relationships Develop* (Prentice-Hall, 1985); Christopher Ryan and Cacilda Jetha, *Sex at Dawn* (HarperCollins, 2010). Alan P. Bell and Martin S. Weinberg, in *Homosexualities* (Simon and Schuster, 1978); Bell and Weinberg found a correlation between a "high level of sexual activity" and "fewer sexual problems" (p. 134). See also Bruce Bagemihl's pioneering book *Biological Exuberance: Animal Homosexuality and Natural Diversity* (St. Martin's Press, 1999), which demolishes the long-standing view that monogamy is characteristic of primate behavior. In their 2002 book, *The Myth of Monogamy*, David Barash and Judith Eve Lipton conclude that monogamy is "not natural"—and certainly "not easy."

8. The findings cited are conveniently summarized in Blake Spears and Lanz Lowen, *Choices: Perspectives of Gay Men on Monogamy, Non-Monogamy, and Marriage* (www.thecouplesstudy.com, 2016).

9. Terence Kissack, "Freaking Fag Revolutionaries: New York's Gay Liberation Front, 1969–1971," *Radical History Review* 62 (1995):

104–34 (Lauritsen, 116); *Come Out!* 1, No. 7 (Dec.–Jan. 1970), quoted in Abram J. Lewis, "'We Are Certain of Our Own Insanity': Antipsychiatry and the Gay Liberation Movement, 1968–1980," *Journal of the History of Sexuality* 25, No. 1 (Jan. 2016): 101; R.D. Laing, *The Politics of Experience* (Pantheon, 1967). See also Christina B. Hanhardt, *Safe Space: Gay Neighborhood History and the Politics of Violence* (Duke University Press, 2013), especially 84–90. In his draft autobiography Allen Young describes the widespread distaste for Lauritsen and O'Brien's "elitist and doctrinaire" attitude (courtesy Young; hereafter cited as Young, manuscript autobiography).

10. Donn Teal, *The Gay Militants* (Stein and Day, 1971); Toby Marotta, *The Politics of Homosexuality* (Houghton Mifflin, 1981).

11. Gary Alinder, "Gay Liberation Meets The Shrinks," *Berkeley Tribe* (May 1970), reprinted in Karla Jay and Allen Young, eds., *Out of the Closets* (Douglas, 1972), 141–45.

12. Alinder, "Gay Liberation Meets The Shrinks"; "A Leaflet for the American Medical Association," and Christopher Z. Hobson, "Surviving Psychotherapy," both in Jay and Young, *Out of the Closets,* 141–45.

13. Kissack, "Freaking Fag Revolutionaries," 120; Red Butterfly, *Gay Oppression: A Radical Analysis* (Red Butterfly, 1970).

14. Abram J. Lewis, "'We Are Certain of Our Own Insanity': Antipsychiatry and the Gay Liberation Movement, 1968–1980," *Journal of the History of Sexuality* 25, No. 1 (Jan. 2016). In this discussion I'm heavily reliant on Lewis's remarkable research and discussion.

15. Ibid., 92.

16. Lauritsen quoted in Kissack, "Freaking Fag Revolutionaries," 119. See also John Stoltenberg, *Refusing to Be a Man* (Breitenbush Books, 1989).

17. Ann Snitow, Christine Stansell, and Sharon Thompson, *Powers of Desire: The Politics of Sexuality* (Monthly Review Press, 1983); Lewis, "'We Are Certain of Our Own Insanity.'"

18. Young, manuscript autobiography.

19. Karla Jay, "Introduction," and Stuart Byron, "The Closet Syndrome," in Jay and Young, *Out of the Closets,* 58–65. The Combahee

statement is reprinted in Barbara Smith, ed., *Home Girls: A Black Feminist Anthology* (Kitchen Table Press, 1983). See also Gloria Anzaldua and Cherrie Moraga, eds., *This Bridge Called My Back: Writings by Radical Women of Color* (Persephone Press, 1981).

20. Byron, "The Closet Syndrome," 60.

21. Young, manuscript autobiography. Young's coeditor Karla Jay also gave communal living a try. Then working toward a PhD in comparative literature, she moved into an Upper West Side apartment with her lover, June Rook, and three gay men—Alan Sample, John Knoebel (one of the founding members of the Effeminists), and the Martha Graham dancer Jude Bartlett (who had an affair with Allen). See Karla Jay, *Tales of the Lavender Menace* (Basic Books, 1999).

22. Radicalesbians (NYC), "Leaving the Gay Men Behind," in Jay and Young, *Out of the Closets*, 290–91; Julie Lee, "Some Thoughts on Monogamy," in Karla Jay and Allen Young, eds., *After You're Out: Personal Experiences of Gay Men and Lesbian Women* (Links, 1975), 44–50.

23. Max Silverstein, "The Politics of My Sex Life," in Jay and Young, *Out of the Closets,* 272–73.

24. Christopher Phelps, "The Closet in the Party: The Young Socialist Alliance, the Socialist Workers Party, and Homosexuality, 1962–1970," *Labor: Studies in Working-Class History of the Americas* 10, No. 4 (2013).

25. John Lauritsen, "The Red Butterfly," and "Gay Oppression: A Radical Analysis," John Lauritsen's website, http://paganpressbooks.com/jpl/TRB.HTM.

26. Young, manuscript autobiography.

27. Simon Watney, "The Ideology of GLF," in Gay Left Collective, ed., *Homosexuality: Power and Politics* (Allison and Busy, 1980).

28. For the early homophile movement, see especially Allan Bérubé, *Coming Out under Fire* (The Free Press, 1990); John D'Emilio, *Sexual Politics, Sexual Communities* (University of Chicago Press, 1983; reprinted, 1998); Marcia M. Gallo, *Different Daughters* (Carroll and Graf, 2006); Jonathan Ned Katz, *Gay American History* (Penguin, 1976); and Toby Marotta, *The Politics of Homosexuality* (Houghton Mifflin, 1981). See Gallo, *Different Daughters,* for the most recent bibliography; and Marc Stein, *Rethinking the Gay and Lesbian Movement* (Routledge, 2012).

29. Hal Tarr, "A Consciousness Raised," in Tommi Avicolli Mecca, ed., *Smash the Church, Smash the State! The Early Years of Gay Liberation* (City Lights, 2009), 22–30.

30. Huey Newton's letter is printed in Mecca, *Smash the Church, Smash the State!* 252–54. My account of the convention, and the quoted remarks, closely follow the versions in Marc Stein, *City of Sisterly and Brotherly Loves: Lesbian and Gay Philadelphia, 1945–1972* (University of Chicago Press, 2000), 330–40; and in Kissack, "Freaking Fag Revolutionaries." See also Lucy Robinson, *Gay Men and the Left in Post-war Britain* (Manchester University Press, 2007).

31. Jay, *Tales of the Lavender Menace*; Stein, *City of Sisterly and Brotherly Loves,* 330–40.

32. The following description of Allen's Cuban experience is partly drawn from his unpublished autobiography; see also his article "The Cuban Revolution and Gay Liberation" in Jay and Young, *Out of the Closets,* 206–28, and his book *Gays under the Cuban Revolution* (Grey Fox, 1981). In an essay I wrote about Cuba at roughly this same time, I express views similar to Young's (see *The Martin Duberman Reader* [The New Press, 2013]), 311–18. See also Emily K. Hobson, *Lavender and Red: Liberation and Solidarity in the Gay and Lesbian Left* (University of California Press, 2016), 70.

33. For a considered view of the treatment of homosexuals in Cuba up through the 1980s, see Lourdes Arguelles and B. Ruby Rich, "Homosexuality, Homophobia, and Revolution," in Duberman, Martha Vicinus, and George Chauncey, eds., *Hidden from History: Reclaiming the Gay and Lesbian Past* (Meridian, 1989), 441–55.

34. Radicalesbians, "Woman-Identified Woman," reprinted in Jay and Young, *Out of the Closets,* 172–77; Charlotte Bunch, "Learning from Lesbian Separatism," in Bunch, *Passionate Politics* (St. Martin's Press, 1987), 182–91. Charlotte and I were members of the founding board of the National Gay Task Force and, along with Betty Powell (now Achebe Betty Powell), formed something of a bond—particularly against "reformist" male board members like Frank Kameny who would periodically rail against the "intrusion" of feminist concerns. I discuss our alliance in my 1996 memoir, *Midlife Queer.* I myself would come to worry about the "reformist" nature of the Task Force, but

during its earliest years (1973–76) it had a number of radical feminists on the board; subsequently it became more centrist.

35. Charlotte Bunch, "Election Year: Gay Perspectives," in Bunch, *Passionate Politics*, 192–95.

36. For more detail, see Alice Echols, *Daring to Be Bad: Radical Feminism in America 1967–1975* (University of Minnesota Press, 1989), especially 210–20.

37. "Can Men and Women Work Together?" in Jay and Young, *After You're Out*, 173–88.

38. "The Effeminists," in Lindsay Branson, "Gay Liberation in New York City," OutHistory, n.d., http://outhistory.org/exhibits /show/gay-liberation-in-new-york-cit/effeminists.

39. "Forum on Sadomasochism," in Karla Jay and Allen Young, eds., *Lavender Culture* (Jove/HBJ, 1978), 85–117; for a defense of S-M see "S and M and the Revolution," *Come Out!* (winter 1972). Most of the words in quotation marks in this and the following paragraph aren't in "Forum," or elsewhere in the literature; they derive from my own reading of the internal debates over sadomasochism that took place in various GLF publications and settings.

40. Martin Duberman, *Stonewall* (Dutton, 1993). My recorded conversations with Sylvia are in the Martin B. Duberman Papers, New York Public Library.

41. Craig G. Harris, "Black, Gay, and Proud," *New York Native* (March 11–14, 1985). See also Gloria Anzaldua, *La Frontera/Borderlands* (Aunt Lute Books, 1987); Joseph Beam, *In the Life* (Alyson, 1986); Essex Hemphill, *Brother to Brother* (Alyson, 1991); Barbara Smith, *Home Girls* (Kitchen Table Press, 1983); and Moraga and Anzaldua, *This Bridge Called My Back*.

42. Thomas Dotton, "Nigger in the Woodpile," in Jay and Young, *After You're Out*, 218–26. See also Jon L. Clayborne, "Blacks and Gay Liberation," and Anita Cornwell, "Three for the Price of One: Notes from a Gay Black Feminist," reprinted in Jay and Young, *Lavender Culture*, 458–76.

43. Allen Young, "Out of the Closets, Into the Streets," in Jay and Young, *Out of the Closets*, 7–14.

44. Young, manuscript autobiography.

45. Dr. Simon Crouch, quoted in Sabrina Bachai, "Study Finds Same Sex Couples Make Better Parents: Is It Because They're More

Prepared?" *Medical Daily,* July 7, 2014, http://www.medicaldaily
.com/study-finds-same-sex-couples-make-better-parents-it-because-
theyre-more-prepared-291628.

46. Mark Joseph Stern, "The Scientific Debate over Same-Sex
Parenting Is Over," *Slate,* April 13, 2016, http://www.slate.com/blogs
/outward/2016/04/13/scientific_debate_over_same_sex_parenting_is_
over.htm

47. Bella DePaulo, *How We Live Now: Redefining Home and Family in
the 21st Century* (Beyond Words, 2015).

48. Hugh Ryan, "Mapping the Family Possible," *Los Angeles Review
of Books* (Sept. 26, 2015).

49. Hugh Ryan, "We Didn't Queer the Institution of Marriage; It
Straightened Us," and "Our Three-Way Relationship Isn't Your Business; Even If We're Doing Business," *The Guardian* (June 29 and Oct.
25, 2014).

50. Lisa Kron, quoted in *New York Times,* June 27, 2015.

51. Marcia M. Gallo, *Different Daughters* (Carroll and Graf, 2006),
passim. For an excellent discussion of Antonio Gramsci's definitions of
subaltern and *hegemonic,* see Kate Crehan, *Gramsci's Common Sense:
Inequality and Its Narratives* (Duke University Press, 2016).

52. Rita Mae Brown, "Queen for a Day," in Jay and Young, *Lavender
Culture,* 76.

53. Julie Lee, "Some Thoughts on Monogamy," in Jay and Young,
After You're Out, 44–50.

TWO. LOVE, WORK, SEX

1. Most of the quotations in this and the following few paragraphs
come from Jim Downs, *Stand By Me* (Basic Books, 2016).

2. See Gordon W. Allport's classic *The Nature of Prejudice* (Beacon
Press, 1954; 25th anniversary ed., Basic Books, 1979); and Lynne M.
Jackson, *The Psychology of Prejudice* (American Psychological Associa-
tion, 2011).

3. James Surowiecki, "The Mobility Myth," *New Yorker* (Mar. 3, 2014).

4. HRC, *Beyond Marriage Equality: A Blueprint for Federal Non-
discrimination Protections* (pamphlet, 2017); Karen Ocamb, "Human Rights

Campaign Launches $26 Million Campaign for 'Grassroots,'" *Los Angeles Blade,* July 11, 2017, http://www.losangelsblade.com/2017/07/11/human-rights-campaign-launches-26-million-campaign-grassroots-army/.

5. Michael Warner, *The Trouble with Normal* (The Free Press, 1972), 90.

6. Ibid., 105 ("will to naiveté"). See also the 2006 statement and petition "Beyond Same-Sex Marriage: A New Strategic Vision for All Our Families and Relationships," *MRonline,* posted Aug. 8, 2006, https://mronline.org/2006/08/08/beyond-same-sex-marriage-a-new-strategic-vision-for-all-our-families-relationships/.

7. As quoted in Warner, *Trouble with Normal,* 113.

8. Katherine Franke, *Wedlocked: The Perils of Marriage Equality* (New York University Press, 2015), 7, 9, 13.

9. *New York Times,* June 23 and July 18, 2017.

10. Franke, *Wedlocked,* 61.

11. Rich Yeselson, "At Labor's Crossroads," *The Nation* (March 27, 2017); "Workplace Discrimination: The LGBT Workforce," *Huffington Post* (June 22, 2016).

12. Anne Balay, *Steel Closets: Voices of Gay, Lesbian, and Transgender Steelworkers* (University of North Carolina Press, 2014); see also Kitty Krupat and Patrick McCreery, *Out at Work* (2000), and Tami Gold's film of the same name.

13. Howard Brick and Christopher Phelps, *Radicals in America* (Cambridge University Press, 2015); Lucy Robinson, *Gay Men and the Left in Post-War Britain* (Manchester Univ. Press, 2007); Hobson, *Lavender and Red.*

14. Duberman, "Cuba," 317.

15. Ryan Conrad ed., *Against Equality: Queer Critiques of Gay Marriage* (Against Equality Publishing Collective, 2010; reissued in a much expanded version by AK Press, 2014); see especially the essays by Martha Jane Kaufman and Katie Miles, Yasmin Nair, and John D'Emilio.

16. Roger Lancaster, "The New Pariahs: Sex, Crime, and Punishment in America," in David M. Halperin and Trevor Hoppe, eds., *The War on Sex* (Duke University Press, 2017). The entire volume is an

invaluable source of information for many of the issues I discuss here; in particular, I'd single out Judith Levine's "Sympathy for the Devil: Why Progressives Haven't Helped the Sex Offender, Why They Should, and How They Can" (pp. 126–73).

17. Maurice Tomlinson, "The New War on Sex: A Report from the Global Front Lines," in Halperin and Hoppe, *The War on Sex*, 409–28.

18. Judith Levine, "Sympathy for the Devil," 126–73; David M. Halperin, "Introduction," in Halperin and Hoppe, *The War on Sex*, 14–16.

19. *New York Times Magazine* (Sept. 11, 2016).

20. American anthropologist Walter Cline, quoted in Amara Das Wilhelm, *Tritiya-Prakriti: Understanding Homosexuality, Transgender Identity, and Intersex Conditions through Hinduism* (Xlibris, 2003).

21. Gerald Hannon, "Gay Youth and the Question of Consent," *Body Politic* (Sept., Nov. 1976). In a subsequent piece, "Men Loving Boys Loving Men" (*Body Politic* [Nov. 1977]), Hannon focused on three men involved sexually with underage (but postpubescent) males. The article resulted in the Toronto police raiding the magazine's office and seizing its subscription lists. A series of arrests and trials followed—Hannon was charged with "criminal obscenity"—that dragged on for several years and eventuated in the exoneration of both Hannon and the *Body Politic* from the charges of distributing "immoral, indecent or scurrilous material." The *Body Politic* lasted until 1987. Tellingly, Jim Downs, in his *Stand By Me*, attacks Hannon's 1977 article for having "conflated sex with mentorship and confused romance with support" and excoriates him for having "never suggested that the boys might not have been equipped to make decisions for themselves." In contrast, Downs entirely fails to raise his voice in calling attention to the racial segregation that did and still does define gay community spaces.

22. Joseph Epstein, "Homo/Hetero: The Struggle for Sexual Identity," *Harper's* (Sept. 1970).

THREE. EQUALITY OR LIBERATION?

1. Michelangelo Signorile, *It's Not Over: Getting beyond Tolerance, Defeating Homophobia, and Winning True Equality* (Mariner Books, 2015);

"Georgia and Bigotry Against Gays," *New York Times*, Feb. 27, 2016; "LGBT Youth," Centers for Disease Control and Prevention (last update June 21, 2017), https://www.cdc.gov/lgbthealth/youth.htm; Alyssa Rosenberg, "In Three Years, LGBT Americans Have Gone from Triumph to Backlash," *Washington Post*, Jan. 25, 2018.

2. Kenji Yoshino, *Covering: The Hidden Assault on Our Civil Rights* (Random House, 2006).

3. Long Doan, Annalise Loehr, and Lisa R. Miller, "Formal Rights and Informal Privileges for Same-Sex Couples," *American Sociological Review* 79, No. 6 (Nov. 2014).

4. Jane E. Brody, "The Challenges of Male Friendships," *New York Times* (June 28, 2016).

5. The ensuing discussion owes a great deal to the essays that constitute Conrad's *Against Equality* (the second, much expanded edition, published in 2014); though the entire volume is eye-opening. I've found particularly enlightening the essays by Yasmin Nair, Dean Spade, Craig Willse, John D'Emilio, Liliana Segura, and Mattilda Bernstein Sycamore. I'm also heavily indebted to Joseph Nicholas DeFilippis's pathbreaking doctoral dissertation, "A Queer Liberation Movement? A Qualitative Content Analysis of Queer Liberation Organizations, Investigating Whether They Are Building a Separate Social Movement" (Portland State University, 2015), courtesy of DeFilippis. In my view, *the* pioneering work in regard to "queering" the gay agenda was Michael Warner's *The Trouble with Normal* (1993)—still very much relevant to ongoing discussions. Of the national organizations, GLAAD, under the leadership of Janson Wu, is doing the most to address intersectional issues.

6. DeFilippis's dissertation will, in revised form, be published sometime in 2018–19.

7. Andrew Sernatinger and Tessa Echeverria, "An Interview with Alan Sears," *New Politics* (Nov. 6, 2013).

8. Kate Redburn, "After Gay Marriage," in Sarah Leonard and Bhaskar Sunkara, eds., *The Future We Want: Radical Ideas for a New Century* (Metropolitan, 2016), 125–35.

9. Dean Spade, "Their Laws Will Never Make Us Safer," in Conrad, *Against Equality*, 165–75. See also Dean Spade, *Normal Life* (the expanded, Duke University Press edition, 2015).

10. See David Cole, "The Truth about Our Prison Crisis," *New York Review of Books* (June 22, 2017), which discusses John F. Pfaff's *Locked In* (Basic Books, 2017) and James Forman Jr.'s *Locking Up Our Own* (Farrar, Straus and Giroux, 2017).

11. Along with Spade, "Their Laws Will Never Make Us Safer," see Christina B. Hanhardt's analysis of hate crime legislation in *Safe Space: Gay Neighborhood History and the Politics of Violence* (Duke University Press, 2013), ch. 4.

12. Jos Truitt, "Why I Don't Support Hate Crime Legislation," *Feministing* (2009), http://feministing.com/2009/07/22/why-i-dont-support-hate-crime-legislation/.

13. The literature on prejudice is vast; for starters, see Gordon Allport's classic *The Nature of Prejudice* (Perseus, 1979) and Yasmin Nair, "Why Hate Crime Legislation is Still Not a Solution," in Conrad, *Against Equality*, 199–204.

14. Tara Parker-Pope, "Gay Unions Shed Light on Gender in Marriage," *New York Times* (June 10, 2008); see also, Martin Duberman, "Gayness Becomes You," *The Nation* (May 20, 2002).

15. For a summary of the research, see Ilan H. Meyer and Mary E. Northridge, eds., *The Health of Sexual Minorities: Public Health Perspectives on Lesbian, Gay, Bisexual, and Transgender Populations* (Springer, 2007).

16. Toby Manning, "Gay Culture: Who Needs It?" in Mark Simpson, ed., *Anti-Gay* (Freedom Editions, 1996) (Manning's emphasis). I also recommend another fine essay in the collection, the novelist John Weir's "Going In."

17. Michael Hobbes, "The Epidemic of Gay Loneliness," *Huffington Post* (March 3, 2017).

18. Emily A. Greytak et al., "Effectiveness of School District Antibullying Policies in Improving LGBT Youths' School Climate," *Psychology of Sexual Orientation and Gender Diversity* 3, No. 4 (2016): 407; see also Greytak et al., "Preparing School Counselors to Support LGBT Youth," *Professional School Counseling* 20, No. 1a (2017): 13–20. On drug addiction, see Perry Halkitis, *Methamphetamine Addiction: Biological Foundations, Psychological Factors, and Social Consequences* (American Psychological Association, 2009), 16–19.

19. As quoted in my article "Bisexuality," *New Times* (June 28, 1974). I rely heavily on this article for the discussion that follows.

20. Charles M. Blow, "Sexual Attraction and Fluidity," *New York Times* (Sept. 7, 2015).

21. Dennison's essay is in Judd Marmor, ed., *Sexual Inversion: The Multiple Roots of Homosexuality* (Basic Books, 1965).

22. Joan Roughgarden, *Evolution's Rainbow: Diversity, Gender, and Sexuality in Nature and People* (University of California Press, 2004). See also the pioneering studies in primatology by Jane Goodall, Diane Fossey, Jane B. Lancaster, and Sarah Blaffer Hrdy—much of it summarized in Meredith F. Small, ed., *Female Primates: Studies by Women Primatologists* (Alan R. Liss, 1983).

23. Duberman, "Bisexuality," in Duberman, *About Time: Exploring the Gay Past* (Meridian, 1991), 291.

24. Clellan S. Ford and Frank A. Beach, *Patterns of Sexual Behavior* (Eyre & Spottiswoode, 1965).

25. See, for example, David M. Halperin, *One Hundred Years of Homosexuality* (Routledge, 1990); John J. Winkler, *Constraints of Desire* (Routledge, 1990); K.J. Dover, *Greek Homosexuality* (Harvard University Press, 1978); Dolores Klaich, *Woman + Woman: Attitudes toward Lesbianism* (Morrow, 1974); and Reay Tannahill, *Sex in History* (Cardinal, 1989).

26. William H. Masters and Virginia E. Johnson, *Homosexuality in Perspective* (Little, Brown, 1979).

27. Duberman, "Masters and Johnson," *New Republic* (June 16, 1979).

28. Rachel Feltman, "Same-Sex Experiences Are on the Rise, and Americans Are Increasingly Chill about It," *Washington Post* (June 1, 2015).

29. Nico Lang, "Why Men's Sex Lives Are More Complicated Than You Might Think," *Daily Dot* (Jan. 30, 2015), http://www.dailydot.com/via/mostly-straight-men-sexual fluidity/; Benedict Carey, "Straight, Gay or Lying? Bisexuality Revisited," *New York Times* (July 5, 2005); Neil Swidey, "What Makes People Gay? (An Update)," *Boston Globe* (Aug. 23, 2015).

30. Alex Therrien, "No Woman 'Totally Straight,' Study Says," *BBC News* (Nov. 6, 2015), http://www.bbc.com/news/health-34744903.

31. Justin Lehmiller, *Sex and Psychology* (blog), http://www.lehmiller.com/blog/2014/2/24 (Sept. 17, 2016). Neil Swidey, "What Makes People Gay?" *Boston Globe* (Aug. 23, 2015), reports that at the 2015 Lethbridge conference, The Puzzle of Sexual Orientation, he was struck at "the new appreciation for [male] fluidity."

32. Joe Kort, "Going with the Flow: Male and Female Sexual Fluidity," *Huffington Post* (Sept. 17, 2016).

33. This binary terminology, I realize, is currently highly contested, and with good reason. But it's the language employed by the researchers I'm citing. When I shift subjects, I shift terminologies as well.

34. Elizabeth Jane Ward, *Not Gay: Sex between Straight White Men* (New York University Press, 2015).

35. Rebecca M. Jordan-Young, *Brain Storm: The Flaws in the Science of Sex Differences* (Harvard University Press, 2010), 4 (citing Patricia Hausman, "A Tale of Two Hormones," www.patriciahausman.com/speeches.html), and 9 (citing Ehrhardt and Baker, "Fetal Androgen…," in R.C. Friedman et al., eds., *Sex Differences in Behavior*).

36. This and the following two paragraphs are based on Jordan-Young, *Brain Storm*, 49–54, 72–75.

37. Ibid. 106–14.

38. Randolph Trumbach, "The Birth of the Queen: Sodomy and the Emergence of Gender Equality in Modern Culture, 1660–1750," in Duberman, Vicinus, and Chauncey, *Hidden from History*, 129–40.

39. Ibid., 258, 278–90 (for this and the following paragraph).

40. Ibid., 185–97.

41. David Valentine, *Imagining Transgender: An Ethnography of a Category* (Duke University Press, 2007).

42. Richard A. Friedman, "How Changeable Is Gender?" *New York Times* (Aug. 22, 2015). In support of his views, Friedman, in turn, cites the earlier work of Richard Green (*The Sissy Boy Syndrome,* [Yale University Press, 1987]), which purportedly found that of the forty-four boys he studied, only one continued to feel gender dysphoria into adolescence and adulthood. (Green, it should be noted, had earlier argued forcefully in favor of declassifying homosexuality as a mental disorder.) Friedman also relies for support of his views on Madeline S.C. Wallein's work (at the VU University Medical Center in the Netherlands)

with seventy-seven gender-dysphoric young people (ages five to twelve); in a follow-up study ten years later, Wallein found that 70 percent of the boys and 36 percent of the girls had "outgrown" their dysphoria. For a historical perspective on transgender identity, a good place to start would be Mark Sameth, "Is God Transgender?" *New York Times* (Aug. 13, 2016). In this op-ed Sameth cites passage after passage in the Hebrew Bible where an elastic view of gender is expressed—for example, Genesis 3:12 (where Eve is referred to as "he") and Genesis 1:27 (which refers to Adam as "them").

43. See, for example, Brynn Tannehill's critique "How to Spot Anti-trans Concern Trolls," *The Blog, Huffington Post,* last updated Aug. 29, 2016, https://www.huffingtonpost.com/brynn-tannehill/how-to-spot-antitrans-con_b_8055816.html.

44. A Dutch study reported in the *New York Times* (Jack Turban, "Hannah Is a Good Girl: Doctors Finally Treat Her like One," April 8, 2017) found that of fifty-five transgender teens given puberty blockers to delay surgery, "none changed their minds and none regretted treatment. All went on to cross-sex hormones around age 16 and later gender-affirming surgery ... by the end, metrics of happiness and quality of life were on a par with those of the general population."

45. Vernon Rosario, "On the Medicalization of Gender," *Gay and Lesbian Review* (Jan.–Feb. 2017). Rosario reviews as well two books skeptical of transgenderism and the medical technologies employed: Bernice L. Hausman's much-contested *Changing Sex: Transsexualism, Technology, and the Idea of Gender* (Duke University Press, 1995) and Bob Ostertag's *Sex, Science, Self: A Social History of Estrogen, Testosterone, and Identity* (University of Massachusetts Press, 2016). In his essay Rosario also expresses a view that in the current climate of opinion will probably bring him grief: "While many transgender people (just as many gay people) like to believe they were 'born this way,' it's an unsubstantiated, inadequate, and unnecessary basis for their gender or sexual identity." Rosario also condemns the term *gender reassignment surgery* as "inaccurate, since surgery and hormones do not reassign but instead confirm the gender that a person has already embraced"; quite reasonably, he prefers the newer term *gender affirming* in regard to hormonal treatment or surgery, but the earlier term has probably been too

widely used to be easily supplanted. In another article ("Quantum Sex: Intersex and the Molecular Deconstruction of Sex," *GLQ: A Journal of Lesbian and Gay Studies* 15, No. 2 [2009]) Rosario provides an intricate and sophisticated discussion about "the enormous complexity of Mammalian sex determination." To give but one example, he reports on the recent work in molecular genetics being done by Phoebe Dewing and her colleagues in Eric Vilain's lab, showing that "differential gene expression was evident *before* the embryonic gonads had formed"—which suggests that the establishment of genetic mechanisms of gender identity in the human brain may have "clinical value in assigning gender to neonates with ambiguous genitalia. This line of research also potentially indicates a genetic basis for transsexualism and more broadly gender atypical behavior." Rosario concludes that the findings of "molecular genetics is likely to require a shift from binary sex to quantum sex, with a dozen or more genes each conferring a small percentage likelihood of male or female sex that is still further dependent on micro- and macro-environmental interactions.... Genes are ... in dynamic flux with the immediate environment in which the gene/individual finds itself, which in turn establishes the timing, pattern, and conditions of expression."

46. The Pink Tank quote is from Ryan Conrad, "The Lure of the Gay Gene," *Gay and Lesbian Review* (Jan.–Feb. 2016).

47. Ana Swanson, "The U.S. Is Still Divided on What Causes Homosexuality," *Wonkblog, Washington Post* (March 10, 2015).

48. This and the following paragraph rely on Conrad, "Lure of the Gay Gene"; J. Michael Bailey, Paul L. Vasey, Lisa M. Diamond, et al., "Sexual Orientation, Controversy, and Science," *Psychological Science in the Public Interest* 17, No. 2 (2016): 45–101; J. Michael Bailey and Richard C. Pillard, "A Genetic Study of Male Sexual Orientation," *Archives of General Psychiatry*, 48 (Dec. 1991); William Byne and Bruce Parsons, "Human Sexual Orientation: The Biologic Theories Reappraised," *Archives of General Psychiatry*, 50 (March 1993).

49. Scott L. Hershberger, "A Twin Registry Study of Male and Female Sexual Orientation," *Journal of Sex Research* 34 (1997); Miron Baron, "Genetic Linkage and Male Homosexual Orientation," *British Medical Journal* 307 (Aug. 7, 1993). To my mind, the most nuanced

book-length study remains Vernon A. Rosario, ed., *Science and Homosexualities* (Routledge, 1997), especially the editor's introduction and the essay by Jennifer Terry.

50. The genetic issue is in fact far from dead. At the 2015 Lethbridge conference, psychiatrist Alan Sanders announced his finding—in seeming confirmation of Dean Hamer's earlier study of Xq28—that gay brothers share genetic markers on their X chromosome. See online "LGBT Science," an ongoing project of Wayne Besen's *TWO: Truth Wins Out.*

51. Eric Anthony Grollman, "Sexual Orientation Differences in Attitudes about Sexuality, Race, and Gender," *Social Science Research* 61 (Jan. 2017): 126–41.

52. Michael Schulson, "Of Politics, Science, and Gender Identity," July 18, 2017, archived at *Undark: Truth, Beauty, Science,* https://undark .org/article/gender-lgbtq-paul-mchugh-science/.

FOUR. WHOSE LEFT?

1. See http://www.hrc.org/.

2. Michelangelo Signorile, "How the Human Rights Campaign Is Helping the GOP to Retain the Senate," *The Blog, HuffPost,* Mar. 25, 2016, https://www.huffingtonpost.com/michelangelo-signorile/how-human-rights-campaign-helping-the-gop_b_9545778.html.

3. "An L.G.B.T. Hunger Crisis," *New York Times,* July 19, 2016.

4. See Harold Meyerson's shrewd analysis of the Sanders phenomenon in "The Long March of Bernie's Army," *American Prospect* (Spring 2016). See also Mark Schmitt, "Is the Sanders Agenda Out of Date?" *New York Times,* June 16, 2016; and Walter G. Moss, "What Do Democratic Socialists like Bernie Sanders Believe?" *History News Network,* April 24, 2016, http://historynewsnetwork.org/article/162541.

5. Warren, quoted in Schmitt, "Is the Sanders Agenda out of Date?" *New York Times,* June 16, 2016.

6. Duberman, introduction to Hans Magnus Enzensberger, *The Havana Inquiry* (1974), reprinted in Duberman, *Left Out: The Politics of Exclusion; Essays, 1964–1999* (Basic Books, 1999), 131–41.

7. Leonard and Sunkara, eds., *The Future We Want* (Metropolitan, 2017); see, as well, Sunkara, *The ABCs of Socialism* (Verso, 2017).

8. *New York Times* (Sept. 4, 2017). On comparable conditions in Russia, see Masha Gessen, "Forbidden Lives," *New Yorker* (July 3, 2017). For more on ILGA, a good start is Dennis Altman, *The End of the Homosexual?* (University of Queensland Press, 2013).

9. See "HRC Foundation," Human Rights Campaign, n.d., https://www.hrc.org/hrc-story/hrc-foundation.

10. John D'Emilio, "Can the Left Ignore Gay Liberation?" *New Politics* (summer 2008): 28–31.

11. Regina Kunzel, "Lessons in Being Gay: Queer Encounters in Gay and Lesbian Prison Activism," *Radical History Review,* No. 100 (winter 2008): 11–37.

12. Mike Riegle, "Sexual Politics of 'Crime': Inside and Out" (November 19, 1983) in Robert B. Ridinger, ed., *Speaking for Our Lives: Historic Speeches and Rhetoric for Gay and Lesbian Rights (1892–2000)* (2004; reprint, Routledge, 2012).

13. Deron Dalton, "The Three Women behind the Black Lives Matter Movement," *Madame Noire,* May 4, 2015, http://madamenoire.com/528287/the-three-women-behind-the-black-lives-matter-movement/; Orie Givens, "Lesbian Black Lives Matter Leader Will Spend 72 More Days in Jail for 'Lynching,'" *Advocate,* June 7, 2016, https://www.advocate.com/crime/2016/6/07/lesbian-black-lives-matter-leader-will-spend-72-more-days-jail-lynching.

14. Heather Boushey, *Finding Time: The Economics of Work-Life Conflict* (Harvard University Press, 2016).

15. Naomi Klein, *No Is Not Enough: Resisting Trump's Shock Politics and Winning the World We Need* (Haymarket Books, 2017).

16. *New York Times,* May 16, July 12, 2016 (schools); Sarah Ruiz-Grossman, "Most Americans Oppose White Supremacists, but Many Share Their Views: Poll," *Black Voices* (blog), *HuffPost* (Sept. 15, 2017).

17. Carol Graham: *Happiness for All? Unequal Hopes and Lives in Pursuit of the American Dream* (Princeton University Press, 2017).

18. *The Nation,* March 7, 2016.

19. Steve Fraser, *The Age of Acquiescence: The Life and Death of American Resistance to Organized Wealth and Power* (Little, Brown, 2015). See also George Scialabba's brilliant review in *The Nation,* May 25, 2015.

20. Stephanie Coontz, "Can the Working Family Work in America?" *American Prospect* (May 17, 2016), 95–99.

21. Peter H. Lindert and Jeffrey G. Williamson, *Unequal Gains: American Growth and Inequality since 1700* (Princeton University Press, 2016).

22. David Leonhardt, "The American Dream, Quantified at Last," *New York Times* (Dec. 11, 2016); Eduardo Porter and Patricia Cohen, "A Bigger Pie, but Uneven Slices" (two articles), *New York Times* (Dec. 7, 2016); Robert Kuttner, "The New Inequality Debate," *American Prospect* (Winter 2016).

23. Nicholas Kristof, "America the Unfair?" *New York Times* (Jan. 21, 2016); Kathryn Edin and H. Luke Shaefer, *$2.00 a Day: Living on Almost Nothing in America"* (Houghton Mifflin Harcourt, 2015); Monica Potts, "The Social Safety Net Doesn't Exist in America," *The Nation* (Oct. 31, 2016).

24. Eric Alterman, "Hungry and Invisible," *The Nation* (Nov. 13, 2017).

25. Bryce Covert and Mike Konczal, "Ending Welfare Reform as We Know It," *The Nation* (Oct. 10, 2016).

26. *The Guardian* (Sept. 23, 2016).

27. *New York Times* (Feb. 21, 2016); Nicholas Kristof, "A History of White Delusion," *New York Times* (July 14, 2016).

28. Walter Scheidel, *The Great Leveler: Violence and the History of Inequality from the Stone Age to the Twenty-First Century* (Princeton University Press, 2017).

29. Jane McAlevey, *No Shortcuts: Organizing for Power in the New Gilded Age* (Oxford University Press, 2016).

30. Andy Stern, with Lee Kravitz, *Raising the Floor: How a Universal Basic Income Can Renew Our Economy and Rebuild the American Dream* (PublicAffairs, 2016).

31. See the analysis in Charles M. A. Clark, "Promoting Economic Equity in a 21st Century Economy: The Basic Income Solution" (USBIG Discussion Paper No. 29, March 2002). An argument for a

more modest guaranteed income, at least in the beginning, see Philippe Van Parijs and Yannick Vanderborght, *Basic Income* (Harvard University Press, 2017).

32. Leonard and Sunkara, *The Future We Want*, 181–82.

33. Redburn, "After Gay Marriage," 125–35. According to *2014 Tracking Report: Lesbian, Gay, Bisexual, Transgender and Queer Grantmaking by U.S. Foundations* (compiled by Funders of LGBTQ Issues, https://www.lgbtfunders.org/wp-content/uploads/2016/05/2014_Tracking_Report.pdf), not since 2009 have so few funders supported LGBTQ issues. Among the report's significant findings is that sixty-two of the largest one hundred foundations in the United States provide no funding specifically focused on LGTBQ communities; funding for HIV-AIDS has nearly doubled while it has *decreased* overall (to a five-year low) for communities of color, for children and youth, and for the trans and bisexual communities. In all of this, the foundation world is reflecting the priorities of the gay mainstream movement itself—from where the bulk of the grant proposals originate.

34. This and the following few paragraphs draw upon Omar G. Encarnación, "The Global Backlash against Gay Rights: How Homophobia Became a Political Tool," *Foreign Affairs* (May 2, 2017), https://www.foreignaffairs.com/articles/2017-05-02/global-backlash-against-gay-rights. See also Jennifer Bendery and Michelangelo Signorile, "Everything You Need to Know about the Wave of 100+ Anti-LGBT Bills Pending in States," *HuffPost* (April 15, 2016), https://www.huffingtonpost.com/entry/lgbt-state-bills-discrimination_us_570ff4f2e4b0060ccda2a7a9; Choe Sang-Hun, "South Korean Military Is Accused of Cracking Down on Gay Soldiers," *New York Times* (April 27, 2017); Andrew E. Kramer, "Chechnya's Anti-gay Pogrom: 'They Starve You, They Shock You,'" *New York Times* (April 23 and May 18, 2017); Masha Gessen, "When Putin Declared War on Gay Families, It Was Time for Mine to Leave Russia," *Slate* (May 15, 2014); Gessen, "Forbidden Lives: The Gay Men Who Fled Chechnya's Purge," *New Yorker* (July 3, 2017); and Gessen, *The Future Is History: How Totalitarianism Reclaimed Russia* (Riverhead Books, 2017).

35. See the important, inclusive anthology edited by Halperin and Hoppe, *The War on Sex*.

36. Jonathan Matthew Smucker, *Hegemony How-To: A Roadmap for Radicals* (AK Press, 2017).

37. Peter Frase, *Four Futures: Life after Capitalism* (Verso, 2016).

38. Gorz as quoted in *Four Futures,* 53–54.

39. Daniel Boyarin, *Unheroic Conduct: The Rise of Heterosexuality and the Invention of the Jewish Man* (University of California Press, 2017). I derive much of the discussion that follows, and now and then directly quote from, my concluding essay in *The Martin Duberman Reader.*

40. Richard Rambuss, "After Male Sex," in Janet Halley and Andrew Parker, eds., *After Sex? On Writing since Queer Theory* (Duke University Press, 2011), 192–204.

41. Parker-Pope, "Gay Unions Shed Light on Gender in Marriage."

Index